Beautiful? I'm

Why Can't I *See* It?

ATE PUBLISHING
    & Enterprises

*B*I'm *eautiful?*
Why Can't I *See* It?

DAILY ENCOURAGEMENT TO
Promote Healthy Eating & Positive Self-Esteem

by KIMBERLY DAVIDSON

TATE PUBLISHING & *Enterprises*

Dedication

To my Father and His Son, Jesus Christ, I give You all the glory. Thank you for allowing me to be your clay, an inspired vessel of Your love. To my husband, Dennis, who had a hard time grasping the nature of an eating disorder, thank you for your support—not only with this project, but with women's ministry in general.

With Gratitude

I am so grateful to all the leaders and teachers who have influenced this book and ministry, Olive Branch Outreach. You have shaped my life by helping me to learn the real truths. I thank God for the ability to now share that knowledge with others.

Thank you, Dr. Gregory Jantz, for being a mentor and supporter of this project. Your encouraging words became part of daily my armor as I navigated through new territory. Thank you, Pastors Scott Delbridge and Larry Bingham, for your support and sermon messages. As you read this book, you will see familiar words.

Thank you, women (you know who you are), for trusting me to help and guide you through the healing process. You will never know how much I've learned from you, and admire each and every one of you.

"It is the Father, living in me, who is doing his work"
(John 14:10).

Table of Contents

Foreword

I've spent the last twenty-two years of my life working with those struggling with an eating disorder. Often, it's difficult for them to put into words what they're feeling and fearing. So, it's important when a book comes along with an authentic voice of one who has emerged whole from the struggle. Kimberly Davidson speaks with such a voice. With the help of a dedicated, courageous group of women, Kimberly has tested these materials. Real people, with real struggles, have worked through these pages and provided input, insight, and inspiration.

This is a structured book, designed to provide a pathway along the recovery journey, without dictating every individual step. She knows that, just as each person is different, each journey will be different, and allows the reader to find their own line along the path.

It is also a book of accountability. There is no pretense here. Her chapters are pointed and poignant. *Chapter Five: Your Mind Is the Battlefield* really captures the importance of having a plan to renew your mind as an essential part of recovery. It captures the essence of Romans 12:2, "Do not conform any longer to the pattern of this world, but be transformed by the renewing of your mind. Then you will be able to test and approve what God's will is—his good, pleasing and perfect will." Through these pages, Kimberly takes you on a journey of mind, spirit, and body renewal. *Chapter Nine: Freedom through Forgiveness* is a powerful key to keep the reader headed in the right direction through the twists and turns of recovery. As a professional eating disorder specialist, I know the power and freedom possible when a person breaks through to forgiveness. Though the concept of forgiveness is often misunderstood, Kimberly beautifully weaves its thread throughout this book.

Woven also throughout this book is an emphasis and reliance upon God's word. Kimberly recognizes how powerful it is when God speaks truth into our lives and allows us to understand and truly believe it does apply to us. These are more than just refrigerator verses for Kimberly—they are the Words of Life and her desire is to share them with others.

This is a book of truth. Moreover, it is a book of hope. Kimberly has opened up her life and her journey to recovery, not to shout about what she has done, but to celebrate what God has done. The good news of this book is that God can do the same for you. Take the steps. Put aside the strongholds of fear. Embrace what Kimberly has so diligently put together. You will be blessed.

Dr. Gregory L. Jantz, Edmonds, Washington
Author of *Hope, Help and Healing for Eating Disorders*

How to Get the Most Out of this Book

~

"We have this hope as an anchor for the soul, firm and secure" (Hebrews 6:19).

A road paved with hope and joy. Isn't that what we are looking for? When someone says *hope,* we usually think about the future. Or we think that hope is like a wish—we want something to happen immediately. Sometimes it does, sometimes it doesn't. For many of us, our hopes have been shattered. There is no more happiness or joy. The kind of hope and joy we need now is a solid trust in God. It is a sense of absolute certainty that God loves us, cares for us, and will do everything He has promised in the Bible, His Word. Like an anchor, hope in God gives us the strength, joy, and security to heal, one day at a time.

I have come forward to share my journey of hope and joy and some of the most difficult and painful times of my life. God gave me the inner strength to move forward with my life. I began to see opportunity within difficulty, not despair. I was given a second chance to start over. The race was over, but my journey began.

God did a mighty work in healing me, but that's not God's primary intention. He shows His glory and His strength through our weaknesses. The apostle Paul said,

Three different times I begged God to make me well again. Each time he said, "No. But I am with you; that is all you need. My power shows up best in weak people." Now I am glad to boast about how weak I am; I am glad to

be a living demonstration of Christ's power, instead of showing off my own power and abilities (2 Corinthians 12:9–10, TLB).

Out of my weakness, I found the truth. *This is hope.*

A negative body image is just one aspect of the problem. Food is not the real problem, it only hides the symptoms. The goal is to understand and accept yourself as God created you so you can stop the self-destructive behavior.

Disordered eating is complex and usually requires psychological, medical, and nutritional treatment. The healing process can be long and arduous, and some professionals will tell you that disordered eating isn't curable. *This doesn't have to hold for you.* Your past does not have to hold you captive. You can receive a new life in Christ and go on to live in prosperity. Once you realize the magnitude of God's love, it will build up your self-esteem, acceptance, approval, and confidence. *This is hope.*

I have seen God heal the wounds of food addiction and negative body image that man thought could never be healed. But that's just like the God of the impossible. As the angel said, "For nothing is impossible with God" (Luke 1:37). God is the only one who can show us who we really are. Developing an intimate relationship with God helps us see ourselves the way that He sees us—as His workmanship (Ephesians 2:10).

It is not a coincidence that you found this book. Up to now many of us have tried to satisfy our hunger by abusing food and substances. If you *really* want to relieve your hunger, you must know God, the Father, and His Word in a deeper way. That is the heart of this devotional study; seeing and feeding on the truth, discerning what it means, and applying the truths to your life today. God has given us everything we need to overcome our issues—the Holy Spirit will guide and teach us.

Once you get started, you may realize that you know very little about yourself. This study can be used as a way out of self-destructive behavior and as a way to establish a close relationship with God. The closer your relationship with God becomes the more He will reveal to you about yourself.

Jesus said numerous times in the Bible, "Follow me." He gave us free will. We can choose not to be responsible and make ourselves miserable, or we can seize every opportunity for a better life. Ultimately, we decide if we want to follow. This study is designed to give you hope, courage, and the God-tools for change. A racecar driver once said, "You accomplish victory **step by step,** not by leaps and bounds."

But change usually means turning some mossy rocks over which can be quite painful. I encourage you not to do the study alone but in a church Bible study, support group, and/or with a counselor. You will find that communicating with a close, trusted group will work wonders (and miracles) in your healing.

This study is 12-step compatible. I would caution you to seek professional help if your feelings begin to overwhelm you.

The pain can become so great that we wonder how we can survive if something doesn't change immediately. The good news is we can change. All you need is a sincere desire to change and a willing heart and mind. In this study, God will use all that you learn week-by-week to heal you . . . if you let Him. Be patient. Give God time. You will experience growth in all areas of your life through an increased sense of self-worth and self-esteem. *"Don't quit five minutes before the miracle happens" (Anonymous).* All that you are learning is essential for healing so don't quit. Pray for strength and endurance.

The devotional study is broken down into thirteen chapters (weeks), containing five days of reading material. Each day includes an inspirational saying, perhaps a ☑ writing activity, and one to three reflective questions. Many of you may want to explore Scripture deeper. A Bible study titled "I Want More Bible Food!" is included at the end of each chapter (some choose to come back to the Bible study as they journey through the book for a second time).

Confucius, the Chinese philosopher said, "It does not matter how slowly you go, so long as you **do not stop.**" I suggest you write all your answers and personal thoughts in a journal, so you will need to purchase an inexpensive journal or notebook. If you chose to explore "I Want More Bible Food!" there is space provided to write your answers (if you wish, you can write them in your journal).

In addition to this study, set aside some quality time each day to spend with the Lord. As you do this, you will see your relationship with Him blossom. You are not bound to a religion, but a person. Like any other important person in your life, this relationship requires nurturing and ongoing communication (prayer). Be honest with God (He knows all your thoughts anyway) and pour out your heart to Him. Then listen for His still, quiet voice. He promises to speak to His own children (John 10:4) through His Word.

Author Francine Rivers said, "Go to the hardest place in your life, the place where you don't want to go, and meet God there."[1] God loves you too much to leave you in that hard place. He met me there, and He will do the same for you. Open the door to your heart and let Him in so the healing and restoration process can begin. *He loves you no matter what you have done.*

Jesus said, "Here I am! I stand at the door and knock. If anyone hears my voice and opens the door, I will come in and eat with him, and he with me" (Revelation 3:20). This verse says that we can partner with Jesus and *eat with Jesus.* How would you eat if Jesus walked through your door and joined you for every meal? That is *food for thought.*

God has a purpose and a plan for each one of us if we allow Him to be Lord. It isn't enough to have good intentions; you must have the desire to let Him reside within you and take control. You must earnestly desire healing and be willing to learn to depend on and to trust God. Restoration is possible *if we do it God's way.* Hebrew 4:7 says, "Today, if you hear his voice, do not harden your hearts." There is no problem that God can't handle. The choice is yours. Freedom from bondage is available for all who are willing to hear and receive.

I pray that our Lord will be in your hearts as you trust in Him for your daily nourishment. May you discover God's marvelous love, and may you have the power to understand how wide, long, high, and deep His love for you really is.

There is a time for everything, and a season for every activity under heaven: a time to be born and a time to die, a time to plant and a time to uproot, a time to kill and a time to heal, a time to tear down and a time to build, a time to weep and a time to laugh, a time to mourn and a time to dance, a time to scatter stones and a time to gather them, a time to embrace and a time to refrain, a time to search and a time to give up, a time to keep and a time to throw away, a time to tear and a time to mend, a time to be silent and a time to speak, a time to love and a time to hate, a time for war and a time for peace (Ecclesiastes 3:1–8).

Today is the time. God bless you on your journey of hope and healing through our Lord Jesus Christ.

Preparing for the
Work Ahead

~

1. *Warm up with prayer.* The first thing I learned was to warm up before each exercise session. That's what we need to do each day before we begin our lesson—warm up with prayer. Before you begin reading, ask God to be the only Person in the room with you, and to fill you with His power and Spirit. Then you will be sufficiently receptive to what He wants to teach you for that day.

2. *Quality Time.* Nowadays we all want a quick fix. This devotional study contains important information. Therefore, you should give yourself the necessary time to complete each day's work. *You* are the only one that can feed on God's Word (the Bible). It is necessary to take the time to interact with the text and Scripture, absorb the truths, and allow God to work within you. How long have you been battling your demons? Chances are you said *years.* Try to put aside at least thirty minutes a day to your restoration. Healing is a daily process (long after you finish this study) that comes from a personal relationship with God.

3. *Journaling (writing).* One way to begin breaking down our wall is through journaling. Don't let journaling frighten you. No one will read what you write except you (so grammar and spelling don't count!). Journaling is about putting our thoughts onto paper. It is a tool that enhances our emotional growth and recovery. Many have found journaling helpful in coming to terms with the past or processing fresh pain. This devotional study requires writing many of your answers in a journal. Some people prefer a chart

format in order to pinpoint specific situations that need additional work. Suggested entries:

- Thoughts and Emotions
- Physical Sensations
- What you did; what you could do next time . . .

This is your future. Don't think of this as school. The work is for *you* and your future. As you prepare for this incredible journey, remember that God led you here for a purpose. Ask Him to show you the direction He wants your life to take. Good luck and God bless you on your journey to a new way of living!

> "The chains of habit are too weak to be felt until they are too strong to be broken."
>
> —Samuel Johnson (1709–1784)

Are you ready?

"I'm ready, God, so ready, ready from head to toe, ready to sing, ready to raise a tune: "Wake up, soul! Wake up, harp! Wake up, lute! Wake up, you sleepyhead sun!" I'm thanking you, God, out loud in the streets, singing your praises in town and country. The deeper your love, the higher it goes; every cloud is a flag to your faithfulness. Soar high in the skies, O God! Cover the whole earth with your glory!" (Psalm 57:7–11, Msg)

Let's go!

Defeating The Monster Within

~

Did you know you don't have to be anorexic, bulimic, or a compulsive overeater to be a disordered eater? If you're constantly thinking about food, dieting, exercise, and weight, or perhaps are just an "occasional" binger or purger, this book is for you too. I found a better way to live, and you can too. **The choice to change was mine, but the actual changing was something God would have to do in me.**

An insatiable monster crept into my life unnoticed. When I was seventeen, I lost fifteen pounds by following a food plan and counting calories. I looked terrific! I received compliments and praise—I wanted more. My whole body image became an obsession. Soon after, bulimia became my choice of weight control when I learned I could eat everything I wanted and still lose weight. Deep down, I knew I needed help. Too ashamed to ask anyone, I looked within myself, reading self-help books until I was blue in the face. Eventually, I talked to a couple of professionals. Nothing worked. I was at war with a monster.

Years later, I met God, and He began to pull me out of the battlefield (my bathroom). I took a journey through the Bible and started to mend emotionally. God gradually started changing me from the inside out. I was previously an average businessperson with low-self esteem, struggling to fit in, striving for that "right" look, hoping I came off looking really smart. I *slowly* emerged a leader because God opened my eyes to the internal gifts He'd created in me. Gifts I never saw because my head was in the toilet most of the time.

I knew I couldn't succeed without being empowered by God Himself to give me consistent strength, graciousness, love, and truthfulness. I just couldn't do it alone. I also came to understand that God wasn't going to intrude on my choices. He gave me free will, and if I wanted His power in my life, I had to ask for it and really want it. I became dependant on God.

As God helped me overcome my fearfulness, my self-image and worth began to improve. "I will give you a new heart and put a new spirit in you" (Ezekiel 36:26). I found the truth and I healed. I no longer live in bondage because in Jesus Christ, bondage is destroyed. *Praise God!*

God did not specifically choose me to overcome emotional (disordered) eating and negative body image. Freedom is available for anyone who makes the decision to follow and listen to God. God may use a variety of vehicles to help you—support groups, a counselor, or pastor, but He will always point you to the Bible—His Word—as His vehicle to help you overcome. When I accepted Jesus as my Lord and Savior, I became a new creation. My old ways died and all things became *new* (Isaiah 61:1; 2 Corinthians 5:17). His Word told me I was a beautiful, loved, one-of-a-kind woman. His Word and the help of the Holy Spirit enabled me to claim victory over this monster. Today I look in the mirror and I see F-A-T, a different kind of F-A-T. *Faithful And True* to my Lord!

I made the decision to surrender my life to God and live differently. I let Him fill the holes in my soul. What has been made available to me is available to you. "God, you did everything you promised, and I'm thanking you with all my heart. You pulled me from the brink of death, my feet from the cliff-edge of doom" (Psalm 56:12–13, Msg).

I took back my life after receiving nourishment from the Bible. The healing devotional studies I explored in the past provided the answers to issues I needed to confront. Each study nurtured my relationship with the Father, a precious gift I most likely would not have received through the typical treatment program. I grew to know Jesus Christ as the Healer of my soul. Jesus felt the same emotions and infirmities that I did, although He was without sin. Jesus connected me to the Father through faith. It was Jesus that led me out of the battle with His weapons of love.

Women from around the world have contacted me for Christian-based support, recovery tools, the 12-steps of healing, and inspiration. Many had tried to find help (freedom) and education, only to find resources and books that base healing on one's self and not on God's Word, which is infallible. Others asked for a study guide based on the comprehensive website I developed (www.olivebranchoutreach.com). Olive Branch Outreach was birthed out of my experience of being freed from the bondage of bulimia and substance abuse addiction.

One day, I cried out to God, *What more can I do to help?* He answered my prayer. He led me to write this healing devotional study for those struggling with their identity (self-esteem), compulsive overeating, anorexia, and/or bulimia. The Bible provides the power to do what needs to be done.

I have researched and read numerous books and programs available to Christians suffering from emotional eating. Books written by respected psychologists, by people who successfully recovered, and by authors who are knowledgeable on pain and suffering. Each have a proven solution, but "one size does not *usually* fit all."

After accumulating reams of data, I sifted out the time-tested methods and steps that have helped countless people heal (including myself). That is the heart of this devotional study. I've come to learn first-hand that successful healing comes as a result of looking at the total person—the emotional, physical, spiritual, and relational. The study focuses primarily on the spiritual but touches on the other areas through God's Word. It is a God-tool for people who truly want to change their lives.

You probably feel like I did, that you have lost faith in yourself and the ability to get back to "normal." You don't want to draw from your inner strength anymore—you want to draw from God's strength. He connects with us to instill faith and justly leads us into battle against our monsters.

"This is what the Lord says: *I have heard your prayer and seen your tears; I will heal you*" (2 Kings 20:5). God offers us hope, and joys flows from hope.

"May the God of hope fill you with all joy and peace as you trust in him, so that you may overflow with hope by the power of the Holy Spirit" (Romans 15:13).

Week One: God's Character

~

Who are you?

Maria greeted her family with a smile and tried not to show how much she hurt inside. Today, the doctor told her, once again, to lose weight. She is putting too much stress on her heart and joints. But she loves the comfort that rich foods bring. *I know I'm fat. At least my doctor is honest with me. Everybody else just tells me what a pretty face I have.*

By day Kim is an outgoing sales manager on the move. By night she hides in her apartment and goes on uncontrollable feeding frenzies. Kim learned she could eat everything she wanted and still lose weight with self-induced vomiting and has lived with bulimia for eight years. She swears she'll stop. *Today is the last day.* But she can't beat the cycle.

Anna, a mother of two, loves to cook for her family, but her family barely notices that she doesn't eat her own cooking. Anna is determined to stay thin at any cost, which includes restricting her daily diet to three hundred calories and abusing substances like diet pills, diuretics, and laxatives. Daily her small frame weakens, yet she wants to be thinner. *If I just lose five more pounds, then I'll be truly satisfied and happy.*

Katrina looks in the mirror and sees "repulsive," "fat," "stupid," even though friends tell her she is one of the most intelligent and beautiful girls in her college. *If I'm so beautiful, why can't I see it?*

Perhaps you see yourself in each of these women. I did. I did all I could to hide the secrets and my character flaws from friends, family, and God. But God knew everything about me already. He knows everything about you. But do you know Him? *Not really?*

That's why we're going to talk about God's character first.

The apostle Peter said,

Do you want more and more of God's kindness and peace? *Then learn to know him better and better. For as you know him better, he will give you, through his great power, everything you need for living a truly good life:* he even shares his own glory and his own goodness with us! (2 Peter 1:2–3, TLB).

It's time for change. Let's open our eyes! God will provide the encouragement and patience to persevere. God has the power and the food we need to make all the changes.

Day One: Who is God?

~

What is your current view of God?

Do you know God as your Heavenly Father? If not, recognize He stands ready to adopt *you* into His family. If you have never developed a relationship with God, it may be because you have a distorted, negative relationship with your earthly father. If your earthly father was demanding, abusive, controlling, a perfectionist, you may think of God that way. But that's not true. God is *the perfect Father.*

☑ List in your journal the ten best characteristics you can think of in a great father. We will come back to this list later.

Millions see God as distant and impersonal, but He is not. *God is the picture of love.* 1 John 4:16 says, "God is love." John is *not* saying that God is lovely or loving, but that He *is* love. John also says, "Whoever does not love does not know God, because God is love" (1 John 4:8).

Our common impressions of God may be very different from the God the Bible actually portrays. As you read the Bible, you will see it is one big love letter from God. "I love you!" is said over and over by God. He says, "I am love. That is who I am. Love."

You may think, *No one seems to care or notices what is going on with me, so why should God? He's the God of "big things," like miracles.* Yes, but He loves each one of us *unconditionally*. Each of us was born with an innate desire to be loved unconditionally, but many of us don't feel or have that unconditional love and are in pain.

Jesus said, "For God so loved the world that he gave his one and only Son, that whoever believes in him shall not perish but have eternal life" (John 3:16). Substitute *your name* for *the world*. Accept that God loves you right now, exactly the way you are, no matter what you've done. It's true!

Biblical Nourishment

Just as our physical body needs the proper nourishment, our spiritual life needs sustenance. God has given us a way to feed our spiritual appetite. Knowing God does not come through a program, a self-help book, or going to church once in awhile. Knowing God comes through a special book, the Bible. It is our road map for living.

The Bible is the ongoing story of God's relationship with humanity. Paul told Timothy that "all Scripture is given by inspiration of God," meaning the words are the expression of God's mind, therefore trustworthy (2 Timothy 3:16–17). The Bible, God's Word, is like a compass; it resets our direction and turns us toward God's desired outcome so that we can begin to make healthy decisions and choices. We will learn to trust God and depend upon His Word to guide us to truth and healing. In other words, *the Bible gives us hope.*

What is God Like?

There is no complete answer, yet the Bible gives us plenty of information. *God is like Jesus.* Jesus was God in the flesh. Jesus said, "Anyone who has seen me has seen the Father" (John 14:9). That is why Jesus came into the world, to give us a glimpse of whom the Father is and what He is like. Jesus always wanted His followers to know His Father. The shortest route to knowing the Father is to know His Son.

When we look at Jesus in the Bible, we see a man full of hope, love, faith, miracles, and so much more. We know that God is kind, gentle, just, merciful, and righteous, because we see all these attributes in the life of Christ. "God's voice thunders in marvelous ways; he does great things beyond our understanding. He says to the snow, 'Fall on the earth,' and to the rain shower, 'Be a mighty downpour'" (Job 37:5–6).

> "True faith requires that we believe everything that God has said about Himself, but also that we believe everything He has said about us!"
>
> —A. W. Tozer

God Defines Himself by Who He Is

"I am compassionate" (Exodus 22:27). "I am merciful" (Jeremiah 3:12). "I am your shield" (Genesis 15:1).

God Defines Himself by Saying What He Feels and Thinks

"I love you with an everlasting love. So I will continue to show you my kindness" (Jeremiah 31:3).

God Defines Himself by What He Chooses To Do

"I will give you a new heart and put a new spirit in you" (Ezekiel 36:26).

"So do not fear, for I am with you; do not be dismayed, for I am your God" (Isaiah 41:10).

God is Faithful

God is always true to His promises. He can never draw back from His promises of blessing or of judgment. Since He cannot lie, He is totally steadfast to what He has spoken (Deuteronomy 7:9 and 2 Timothy 2:13). "The Lord is good. He is a fortress in the day of trouble. He knows those who seek shelter in him" (Nahum 1:7).

Reflective Questions

What have you learned about God that you didn't know before? What has God put in your life to show you that He loves you and that you need Him?

What does God mean to you today? How does that differ from yesterday?

Day Two: Attributes of God

∽

It's different with God.

Give God a chance to show you who He really is. Never in your life will God express His will toward you except as perfect love. God will never give you second best like man will. St. Augustine said, "God loves each one of us as though there were only one of us to love." It's true!

> "Maybe you have a hard time believing that God likes you; maybe you don't even like yourself. But it's true. God not only loves you; He likes you."
>
> –Donna Partow[2]

God is "Omniscient": He is All-Knowing

Do you think that God knows *everything* about you, what you are thinking and doing, millisecond by millisecond? God has *perfect knowledge* of everything that is past, present, or future (Job 37:16; Psalm 139:1–6). That means that whenever God expresses Himself to us, we have to be confident that His directions are always right. Job 9:4 says God's "wisdom is profound, his power is vast."

Our issues with food have isolated most of us to our own island. We live in secrecy. We hide our true feelings and real selves. *God knows each secret. He knows everything. He sees everything.*

God is "Omnipotent": He is All-Powerful

God is able to bring into being anything that He has decided to do with or without the use of any means. Psalm 147:5 tells us that "great is our Lord and mighty in power; His understanding has no limit."

God is "Omnipresent": He is Present Everywhere

God is near, far, in heaven, and on earth with us (Proverbs 15:3). Jeremiah 23:23–24 says, "'Am I only a God nearby,' declares the Lord, 'and not a God far away? Can anyone hide in secret places so that I cannot see him?' declares the Lord. 'Do not I fill heaven and earth?' declares the Lord." God is present everywhere, in the entire universe, at all times, in the totality of His character. "Nothing in all creation is hidden from God's sight" (Hebrews 4:13).

Reflective Questions

How does it make you feel that God knows all about you—past, present, and future? What areas of your life are you trying to hide from God?

☑ Now that you know God knows and sees everything, take a moment to write or say a prayer to your Father. Tell Him exactly how you feel

Day Three: The Perfect Father

~

God wants to be *your* Father.

When you hear the word "father," does it give you warm fuzzies or stir up feelings of hurt and bitterness? It may be hard for you to accept God as your Father, especially if you have a broken relationship with your dad. It's not uncommon to hear that our parents weren't around much for us when we were growing up. Even the wisest and most loving parents do not nurture children perfectly; in fact, perfect human parents do not exist.

Or maybe you were physically or emotionally abused. It may be very difficult for you to believe God the Father can love and protect you. Perhaps your parent's love was based on merit, good behavior, or achievement. If you felt you had to earn love, then you probably feel that you need to be this perfect person before God will take a look at you.

God wants to adopt you. To accept adoption by God is to enter into a parent/child relationship that is different than any other. In God, we find the perfect love and wisdom of the perfect Parent. We also become a coheir with our Brother and Savior, Jesus.

> "God has very long sleeves. One never knows what He has up them."
>
> –Christians In Recovery[3]

Our Heavenly Father is always with us—more than an earthly parent is able to. If an absent or abusive parent has gravely wounded you, remember God promises never to leave or forsake you (Hebrews 13:5). His loving Spirit is always available to guide and prompt us. My favorite description of God is given to us in Isaiah 40:28–31:

Do you not know? Have you not heard? The Lord is the everlasting God, the creator of the ends of the earth. He will not grow tired or weary, and his understanding no one can fathom. He gives strength to the weary and increases the power of the weak. Even youths grow tired and weary, and young men stumble and fall; but those who hope in the Lord will renew their strength. They will soar on wings like an eagle; they will run and not grow weary, they will walk and not faint.

That passage provided great comfort as I ventured down my road of healing. I can tell you firsthand, you can soar on wings like an eagle and overcome any abnormal eating patterns.

☑ Take a moment to meditate on this passage. What attributes of God do you want to praise Him for? How has this passage spoken to you?

God is Our Comforter

We can receive such peace when we realize God is with us throughout our entire day. Unfortunately, the world can't see or feel His comfort unless they choose to accept Jesus Christ. When we do, we find His sustaining power and grace.

In John 14, Jesus comforts His disciples. "Praise be to the God and Father of our Lord Jesus Christ, the Father of compassion and the God of all comfort, who comforts us in all our troubles" (2 Corinthians 1:3–4).

God is the Perfect Disciplinarian

God is perfect love, but He will also discipline us. "My son, do not despise the Lord's discipline and do not resent his rebuke *because the Lord disciplines those he loves,* as a father the son he delights in" (Proverbs 3:11–12). God will bring discipline on those who continue to sin and rebel—not out of anger, but loving correction for our own good (Hebrews 12:5–10). But remember, His discipline and commandments are always based on love no matter how He expresses it.

Remember when you were a small child and your parents disciplined you when you ran in front of a car or played with matches? It was in love, and it was for your best interest. There are consequences to all our actions . . . to our sin. God only wants the very best for us without any thought for Himself. "Blessed is the man whom God corrects; so do not despise the discipline of the Almighty. For he wounds, but he also binds up; he injures, but his hands also heal" (Job 5:17–18).

Reflective Questions

If you really believe that God is love, when God says *no,* will you accept the fact that His will is always best for you?

Where does God now fit on your priority list? Can you make a commitment to make God your top priority? If not, what is standing in the way?

Day Four: The Great Physician

~

"Jehovah-Rapha," the God Who Heals.

The God who is in the process of healing the woman with a food addiction or the one abused by her father is the same God that can heal *you*. More than two thousand years ago, Plato wrote, "If the head and body are to be well, you must begin with the soul; that is the first thing."

It is gratifying to see that today science and medicine are recognizing Plato's wisdom by treating addictive diseases with spiritual healing. Our best medical people are following Louis Pasteur's words: "A little science estranges men from God; much science leads them back to him."[4] Medicine owes its greatest debt to Jesus of Nazareth—the great Physician. Time by itself is not a healer. Jesus Christ has the answer for a bruised heart (and body).

> "Jesus said, 'I tell you the truth, if you have faith as small as a mustard seed, you can say to this mountain, 'Move from here to there' and it will move. Nothing will be impossible for you'" (Matthew 17:20).

In Exodus 15:22–26, God revealed a part of His character to His people. God wanted the children of Israel to learn an important principle. He said in verse 26, "If you listen carefully to the voice of the Lord your God and do what is right in his eyes, if you pay attention to his commands and keep all his decrees, I will not bring on you any of the diseases I brought on the Egyptians, for I am the Lord, who heals you." What do we learn? If the Israelites turned back to God, He would heal them.

If we do what God says, we, too, can be healed. Psalm 147:3 tells us that God is the healer of the brokenhearted. "He is the one who bandages their wounds." When things are difficult, run to God. He can take the bitter and make it sweet because He is our Healer.

God is Our Wonderful Counselor

Jesus said the Holy Spirit, our Counselor, would guide us into all truth (John 14:26; 16:3). We are looking for direction out of the hole we've gotten ourselves into. He will never lead us in the wrong direction like mankind will. He will make our paths straight if we trust Him instead of our own intuition (Proverbs 3:5–6).

How does He do that?

1. By His Word (Psalm 119:24)
2. By His Spirit (Acts 16:6–7)
3. By circumstances (Psalm 32:8)
4. By godly people (Proverbs 27:9)

Reflective Questions

What things feel especially heavy to you right now? How can knowing God's character help lighten that load?

What areas of your life are competing for the affection and loyalty that belong to God alone? (Hint: Instead of food, whom should you be running to?) What will you do differently now?

Day Five: Why Develop a Relationship with God?

~

What were we made for?

What aim should we set ourselves in life? To know God. What is the best thing in life, bringing more joy, delight, and contentment than anything else? Knowledge of God . . . Once you become aware that the main business that you are here for is to know God, most of life's problems fall into place of their own accord.[5]

–J.I. Packer

God desires an intimate relationship with us. *Why? He wouldn't like me anyway.* Nothing could be further from the truth. In God's eyes, you are a child He wanted and specially planned for. Isaiah 30:18–19 says so. "Yet the Lord longs to be gracious to you; he rises to show you compassion . . . How gracious he will be when you cry for help! As soon as he hears, he will answer you."

The Bible says to call Him "Father." He can also be addressed as "Abba," which can mean *daddy.* That's an intimate connection. We can be completely open and transparent with Him. We can trust Him with everything—weakness, suffering, requests.

> "Live life with an audience of One (God)."–Os Guinness

In Exodus 15:22–27, the Israelites witnessed miracle after miracle. God protected them from the Egyptian plagues, and He led them out of Egypt. The most miraculous feat was when He shored up the waves of the Red Sea so they could pass. What a good and gracious God! I'm encouraged when I read this story. It reminds me that the battle is not mine but the Lord's battle. Wouldn't you have liked to have seen the Israelites faces and heard their remarks as they witnessed this mighty miracle? They were obviously thrilled. But three verses later, their attitudes changed. Joy turned to bitter water. The Israelites grumbled against Moses, saying, "What are we to drink?"

How soon they forgot God's entire miracle. How could they not trust Him? Don't we do the same? We are slow to point out God's graciousness. We are quick to complain about our life, our family, and our circumstances. We soon doubt the protection and provision of our God.

God told the Israelites in Deuteronomy 4:9, "Only be careful, and watch yourselves closely so that you do not forget the things your eyes have seen or let them slip from your heart as long as you live." That's one verse we should not forget.

The people that related to God best—Abraham, Moses, David, Isaiah, and Jeremiah—treated him with startling familiarity. They talked to God as if He was in the chair next to them. We can too. When we seek God, He accomplishes through us something only He can do. Then we come to know God in a more intimate way because we experience Him at work through us.

When we develop a relationship with God, our values change too. We place a higher premium on relationships and character instead of on body image, beauty, stature, money, or achievements.

After I healed from bulimia, keeping up with the latest trends, fashions, and body images just didn't matter as much. I once thought all these things were so important, but I consider them worthless because of what Christ did for *me*. Jesus said, "This is eternal life: that they may know you, the only true God, and Jesus Christ whom you have sent" (John 17:3). The heart of eternal life is for you to know God and His son, Jesus Christ whom He sent just for *you*.

Many of us with abnormal eating patterns have tried program after program and read self-help books until we're blue in the face. Nothing's worked. Jeremiah 6:14 says, "They dress the wound of my people as though it were not serious." That means we try to heal superficially. These means don't touch our hearts, spirits, or change the inside.

Think about a best friend. What makes your relationship so strong?

Knowing God is also a relationship with a Person. It is an *intimate love relationship*. Right now, you may have a hard time digesting that, but in time you will find it to be true. Oswald Chambers said, "As soon as God becomes real, other people become shadows. Nothing that other saints do or say can ever perturb the one who is built on God."[6]

Did you know the very reason God created mankind was to have someone to give Himself to, someone to love? The reason for your life is to be loved by God.

God is respectfully and patiently waiting for our invitation to let Him in. The human spirit can be reborn from above into a living relationship with God (John 3:3–8). Through the indwelling of the Holy Spirit, we can begin to flourish in the life-giving fruit of the Spirit (Galatians 5:22–23).

Get to know your Father. His phone line is always open: it's J-E-R-E 33:3: "Call to me and I will answer you and tell you great and unsearchable things you do not know."

Reflective Questions

☑ Pull out your list of the ten best characteristics you can think of in a great father. Compare that list to God's characteristics. What does this tell you?

Is there anything to hold you back from trusting God with your problems (family, job, marriage, health) and pain (anger, fear, shame, guilt)?

Complete this sentence: *I have hope in a new life because . . .*

Finale: Week One

~

Aren't rainbows spectacular!

Those spectral colors that appear in the sky opposite the sun are God's creation. He not only created that beautiful rainbow—He is that beautiful rainbow. God gives us everlasting promises in those glorious colors. Each color reminds us of His promises:

1. Red: for His love (John 3:16)
2. Orange: for His warm healing and comfort (Matthew 5:4)
3. Yellow: for the sun (joy) that will shine again in our lives (Jeremiah 31:13)
4. Green: for the growth in our lives (1 Peter 2:2)
5. Blue: for His unending faithfulness and trustworthiness (Psalm 56:3–4)
6. Indigo: we are His children (Luke 20:36)
7. Violet: for a season of singing (Song of Solomon 2:12)
8. White: for His purity and holiness (Psalm 51:7)

Promise to Claim: "For the Lord is good and his love endures forever; his faithfulness continues through all generations" (Psalm 100:5).

As we close Week One, I trust the Holy Spirit has empowered you to feel God's unconditional love, and you are thirsty to learn more. If you haven't given your life to Jesus Christ, you may feel moved to now. *Come just as you are—you don't have to be healed, perfect, or addiction-free.* If you don't feel ready, you can come back to this page when the Holy Spirit moves you to do so. To give your life to Christ (Romans 10:9–14):

A. Admit you are a sinner and ask for forgiveness.

B. Believe that Jesus Christ died for you on the Cross and rose from the grave.

C. Confess that Jesus Christ is the only way to God and commit to live for Him for the rest of your life.

Pray the Prayer of Salvation

Dear Lord Jesus, I do believe You are the Son of God and that You died on the cross to pay the penalty for my sin. Please come into my life, forgive my sin, and make me a member of Your family. I now turn from going my own way. I want You to be the center of my life. Thank You for the gift of eternal life and for Your Holy Spirit who has now come to live in me. I ask this in your name, Amen.

If you have just prayed this prayer, your relationship with God has just begun. The Bible says you are a brand new person, hence the term "born-again." Your old person has gone, and today is a brand new beginning for you.

"How Great Thou Art"
by Carl G. Boberg and R.J. Hughes
O Lord my God! When I in awesome wonder
Consider all the worlds Thy hands have made
I see the stars, I hear the rolling thunder,
Thy power throughout the universe displayed
Then sings my soul, my Savior God to Thee
How great Thou art, how great Thou art
Then sings my soul, my Savior God to Thee
How great Thou art, how great Thou art.

I Want More Bible Food!

Week One: God's Character

~

Psalm 139

What is the greatest hindrance you face in walking with God?

☑ Psalm 139 reveals a lot about God but also tells us about ourselves. As you read this psalm, take note that God made our bodies and that alone makes them wonderful (verse 14). Each of us wears a label, "Handmade by the Lord."

¹ O Lord, you have searched me and you know me. ² You know when I sit and when I rise; you perceive my thoughts from afar. ³ You discern my going out and my lying down; you are familiar with all my ways. ⁴ Before a word is on my tongue you know it completely, O Lord. ⁵ You hem me in—behind and before; you have laid your hand upon me. ⁶ Such knowledge is too wonderful for me, too lofty for me to attain. ⁷ Where can I go from your Spirit? Where can I flee from your presence? ⁸ If I go up to the heavens, you are there; if I make my bed in the depths, you are there. ⁹ If I rise on the wings of the dawn, if I settle on the far side of the sea, ¹⁰ even there your hand will guide me, your right hand will hold me fast. ¹¹ If I say, "Surely the darkness will hide me and the light become night around me," ¹² even the darkness will not be dark to you; the night will shine like the day, for darkness is as light to you. ¹³ For you created my inmost being; you knit me together in my mother's womb. ¹⁴ I praise you because I am fearfully and wonderfully made; your works are wonderful, I know that full well. ¹⁵ My frame was not hidden from you when I was made in the secret place. When I was woven together in the depths of the earth, ¹⁶ your eyes saw my unformed body. All the days

ordained for me were written in your book before one of them came to be.
[17] How precious to me are your thoughts, O God! How vast is the sum of them!
[18] Were I to count them, they would outnumber the grains of sand. When
I awake, I am still with you. [19] If only you would slay the wicked, O
God! Away from me, you bloodthirsty men! [20] They speak of you with evil
intent; your adversaries misuse your name. [21] Do I not hate those who hate
you, O Lord, and abhor those who rise up against you? [22] I have nothing but
hatred for them; I count them my enemies. [23] Search me, O God, and know
my heart; test me and know my anxious thoughts. [24] See if there is any of-
fensive way in me, and lead me in the way everlasting.

☑ Circle all the references to "I," "me," "mine," "my." Put a star
by those you can relate to (personalize). Meditate on this passage.
Put a question mark besides those truths you are not sure you can
believe and then talk to God about each truth.

When we hear "Christ in me," it means that God knows everything
about me.

He knows my name.

He saw me when I was being formed in my mother's womb.

He was there, knitting *me* together!

He knows when I sit down and stand up.

He knows how many hairs on my head

He knows my words completely, even before they are
spoken.

God knows each one of us intimately.

Nothing we do surprises Him.

Nothing we have done or will do in the future can
surprise Him.

He knows our addictive and/or compulsive nature.

He's not pleased with what it has done to us.

He is touched by our struggles and is committed to our
wholeness—just as He was committed to delivering the children
of Israel.

He will lead us through the healing process and "everlasting
way."

Week Two: Pursuing Perfection God's Way

~

Have you *never* felt ugly, insecure, fat, invisible, or unloved, ?

Ever felt like you've been dealt a bad hand? *Everyone* has. That's not surprising. We live in a society that is narcissistically obsessed with physical perfection, is anti-fat, and discourages physical flaws.

Even if you can recite the New Testament, you may be feeling disgusted with your weight. Maybe you just don't feel very pretty. Or maybe people tell you that you are drop-dead gorgeous, but you just feel like a piece of moldy bologna. Have you asked yourself why?

A large part is the images and lies our culture and the media have fed us.

It certainly was a big part of my life. This I've come to know. The images we see in the media are taped, tucked, airbrushed, and altered! Real self-worth and beauty aren't what we see in magazines, romance novels, or on movie screens; it doesn't depend on what our peers say or what our culture currently reflects.

True self-worth and beauty, true perfection, is seeing ourselves as God sees us. We're going to start looking up to Someone real—God. God has made promises to you, and as you study, He will begin to give you a picture of who you really are. *Everyone has beauty but not everyone sees it.*

Day One: Facing What is Real

~

What I'd give to be a super-model!

The boys in my sixth grade class told me I could be a model but only for *Mad Magazine*. I started to create collages of models because they represented "perfection" to me. They became my idols. *Models and actresses give me life!* I turned my heart to idols because I connected with them. An idol is anything, or anyone, we put our trust in in order to meet our needs apart from God. An idol can be described as a *God substitute*.

Isaiah 44:17–18 says, "From the rest he makes a god, his idol; he bows down to it and worships. He prays to it and says, 'Save me; you are my god.' They know nothing, they understand nothing; their eyes are plastered over so they cannot see, and their minds closed so they cannot understand."

Can you see how an idol (perfect person) might be a delusion?

Inevitably, my idols made me feel worthless and humiliated because I couldn't measure up to their standards. *I hate my body!* Why do so many of us hate our bodies? Why aren't we pleased with what God gave us? We cry, "I must be beautiful and perfect!"

We ignore our genetic code. So what happens? Since we can't attain that perfection, we don't feel good about ourselves because our self-esteem has become related to our body and self-image.

When we don't feel good about ourselves, it's hard to develop meaningful relationships with others.

Whatever happened to the importance of "inner beauty?" The Bible says, "Do not consider his appearance or his height, for I have rejected him. The Lord does not look at the things man looks at. Man looks at the outward appearance, but the Lord looks at the heart" (1 Samuel 16:7).

Christ looks at the heart. Why are we all so enslaved to the way we look?

1. We buy into the lies the media feeds us.

Our hearts believe the lies that physical beauty will bring satisfaction and recognition. False promises like, *If I'm beautiful, I will be happy and successful. I'll be popular and desirable to men. I will know lasting intimacy and true love. I'll be secure, important, significant, and confident.*

2. Other factors (besides attaining perfectionism) can contribute to abnormal eating habits.

For example, depression, a dysfunctional family system, control and dependency, performance pressure from the family (especially in the area of grades and other parent appointed activities), involvement in activities that promote thinness like gymnastics, swimming, dancing, cheerleading, running, ice-skating, and appearance-oriented activities like modeling and beauty pageants.

God knows women are interested in making themselves look good. The apostle Peter defines inner beauty for us:

Your beauty should not come from outward adornment, such as braided hair and the wearing of gold jewelry and fine clothes. Instead, *it should be that of your inner self, the unfading beauty of a gentle and quiet spirit, which is of great worth in God's sight.* For this is the way the holy women of the past who put their hope in God used to make themselves beautiful (1 Peter 3:3–5).

What kind of adorning does God think is beautiful in women?Examples of beauty: there is beauty in integrity, intelligence, humor, simplicity, and complexity. Can you think of other examples?

> When a child of God looks into the Word of God, she sees the Son of God and is changed by the Spirit of God into the image of God for the glory of God.
>
> -Anonymous

Reflective Questions
Where Do You Fall on the Perfection Scale?

Circle or underline each statement that you think describes you:

- The more "beautiful" and thin I am, the happier I'll be.

- My appearance will help me achieve my goals and dreams.

- I am fat and ashamed of my appearance.

- I won't be happy until I fix some of my physical characteristics.

- If I eat anything that contains sugar or fat, I'll get fat.

- If I don't have the "right" look, then I won't have the best job, relationships, and, ultimately, happiness.

- I am not a very attractive person.

☑ If you believe any one of these statements, you are perfectionist. They each represent a lie, or wrong assumption, and lead to negative body image.

Make a list of the messages you are currently receiving from the outside (i.e. media, parental, peers, work) that are pushing you to attain perfection.

What is one way you will use today's lesson and Scripture to change your life this week?

Day Two: God's Perfection

~

**Physical beauty does not ensure happiness,
fulfillment, or success.**

The media painted Princess Diana (of England) as the ideal.
She was beautiful, young, rich, and powerful. She was idolized by
millions of women. Yet despite all of that, she was not a happy
person. Throughout history the lives of the most physically attractive women have often been tragic and pitiful (remember Marilyn
Monroe?). Let's go back to the beginning.

Genesis 1:27 says, "God created man in his own image, in the
image of God he created him; male and female he created them."
Think about that. It was through the creation of both man and
woman that God gave us His greatest self-revelation.

After studying God's character last week, does your image of
God bear any resemblance to your self-image? You probably answered no. That's because most of us suffer from low self-image.

"That which is striking and beautiful is not always good; but
that which is good is always beautiful."
—Ninon de l'Enclos[7]

Unconditional Love

In the Bible there are frequent passages about God's unconditional love and people's sins. Time after time, Jesus' disciples
disappointed Him. They quarreled with each other about who was
the most important; they misunderstood His mission; and at the

moment of crisis, they deserted Him. *Yet He never stopped loving them.*

In Hosea 4, Israel had turned her back to God. You would think that God would throw His hands up and say, "I give up on you. You can no longer be my people." But He doesn't. At the end of Hosea 4, God says He will not come in wrath, and that He will settle the Israelites in their home. He loves them so much! These words demonstrate the matchless love of God.

This is how God feels toward you and me—loving us so much, shedding tears with us, feeling our pain, wishing we could feel His love and trust. *God knows we are not perfect, and God doesn't expect us to be perfect.*

The Mask of Perfection

Many of us wear a *mask of perfection.* I did. I needed to please everyone and gain his or her approval. *I must create the perfect body and land the perfect job so that I'll be admired and respected.* Maybe you thought that if you ever did anything wrong that you wouldn't be liked by your parents, friends, or teachers. Maybe you think that if you're not perfect, you won't be loved.

Having extreme rules and standards by which we measure ourselves leads to self-criticism and personal torment. When I *finally* was able to admit I wasn't perfect and could never be perfect, I was admitting *I needed God.* That was a good thing!

But then I read the verse, "Be perfect, therefore, as your heavenly Father is perfect" (Matthew 5;48). I was confused! I consulted my circle of respected pastors and learned that this verse is a summary statement, a review of what Jesus talked about in the Sermon on the Mount.

Jesus told His listeners that they should love not only their neighbors but their enemies as well. "If you love those who love you, what reward will you get?" (Matthew 5:46). Pastor Kenneth Gribble[8] explains:

The word "perfect" is the Greek word *teleios,* and is translated to mean "mature, fully developed." It doesn't refer to moral perfection, but to the kind of love that is like God's love—mature, complete, openhearted to all, full of blessing. So the words in Matthew, "You must be perfect," means *we are to love as God loves, and be whole.*

Perhaps you said to a loved one, *"You want me to succeed, but could you understand if I failed? Could you love me if I failed?"* No matter what we've done or what we'll do, we are a success. If we've set out to do something today and fell short of our goals, we haven't lost the admiration, respect, or love of those around us. There are those who will love us whether we fail or succeed.

Christ died for you and me because we can never be perfect, but better yet, He died so that *we don't have to be perfect!* If you do something ninety-nine percent perfect but still feel you are defective because of the one percent imperfection, this is good news!

☑ Bring to the Lord any perfectionism you are currently experiencing. Ask Him in a prayer to help you overcome those behaviors, and come back daily to your prayer over the week.

Reflective Questions

How can your self-image be low when you were created in the image of God?

Explain this statement in your own words: "Perfectionism leads to unrealistic and unattainable expectations of ourselves."

Day Three: About Sin

~

The Bible is clear about sin.

Sin is a term usually describing lack of conformity to the will of God; especially, willful disregard for the laws revealed in God's Word.

My husband's parents had a Doberman named Duke. They loved this dog and the dog loved them, minding every command. The grandkids would come to visit and play with Duke. One day, Duke turned on little Sonia and disfigured her face, and they had to put Duke down. Duke came into this home and became part of the family. The family cared for and nurtured Duke, and then, quite unexpectedly, Duke turned on them and became the "destroyer."

So it is with sin Sin doesn't appear as sin to us—it entertains, is playful, is educational, and even sleeps with us, but its nature is always the same. Inevitably, it will always rise up to bite and devour those who befriend it.

Sin is anything that violates God's law, or commandments. But how do we understand sin? I believe sin refers to anything that causes brokenness. That means a broken relationship with my family, spouse, friends, God, and myself.

Sin is also called evil. Evil has a name. The most common names are Satan, the enemy, Lucifer, the evil one, and the devil. John 8:42–47 tells us that Satan is the *father of all lies*. He seeks to rule from the realm of the unseen—the spiritual dimension. He uses three tools to deceive us: *deception, isolation,* and *secrecy.* Does that hit home for you?

He wants to drive us into hopelessness by saying our sins are too numerous and horrible. That is the very reason why we need to seek our Savior, His mercy, and His grace. Sin is so important that God sent His only Son, Jesus, to die in order to get rid of sin for once and all.

> "Beauty is mysterious as well as terrible. God and devil are fighting there, and the battlefield is in the heart of man."
>
> –Dostoyevsky[9]

Ruth Bell Graham said there are three steps to sin[10]:
- Contemplation
- Rationalization
- Consent

P.S. Sin always affects others.

Is Emotional Eating a Sin?

All sickness (physical and emotional) is ultimately due to the fallen condition of the world that makes us vulnerable. Emotional eating, addiction, obsession, etcetera, result from these vulnerabilities. It is important that we avoid the blame game and offer one another spiritual guidance and education in order to make healthier personal choices.

What science calls illness or disorder, Scripture explains as the result of the fall of man and the broken condition of the world. Science says our problems are an "illness" and treats them with medicine. Scripture makes it clear there is an element of personal sin involved and offers us accurate moral guidance.

Spiritual Truth

Jesus taught spiritual truth through everyday things. As we observe Jesus in different situations, we can see how He deals with people from other than the world's perspective. What is one principle from this passage you can apply to your life this week? John 8:1–11:

> ¹ *But Jesus went to the Mount of Olives.* ² *At dawn he appeared again in the temple courts, where all the people gathered around him, and he sat down to teach them.* ³ *The teachers of the law and the Pharisees brought in a woman caught in adultery. They made her stand before the group* ⁴ *and said to Jesus, "Teacher, this woman was caught in the act of adultery.* ⁵ *In the Law Moses commanded us to stone such women. Now what do you say?"* ⁶ *They were using this question as a trap, in order to have a basis for accusing him. But Jesus bent down and started to write on the ground with his finger.* ⁷ *When they kept on questioning him, he straightened up and said to them, "If any one of you is without sin, let him be the first to throw a stone at her."* ⁸ *Again he stooped down and wrote on the ground.* ⁹ *At this, those who heard began to go away one at a time, the older ones first, until only Jesus was left, with the woman still standing there.* ¹⁰ *Jesus straightened up and asked her, "Woman, where are they? Has no one condemned you?"* ¹¹ *"No one, sir," she said. "Then neither do I condemn you," Jesus declared. "Go now and leave your life of sin."*

Reflective Questions

Give an example of a sin that you committed without really stopping to contemplate what it would cost you.

What hope does Jesus give you?

Day Four: Denial

~

D = don't; E = even; N = notice; I = I; A = am; L = lying.

Denial is all the things we tell ourselves to rationalize, justify, or minimize our unhealthy patterns. *Everybody deals with weight, image, and food issues. I'm like everyone else.* Denial is a very common emotional reaction when we are confronted with our obsessions about food or our body.

Convincing ourselves that our lives are working successfully is a form of denial. It is a self-protecting behavior that keeps us from honestly facing the truth. Jesus said, "Why do you look at the speck of sawdust in your brother's eye and pay no attention to the plank in your own eye?" (Luke 6:41)

Denial is a powerful tool that the enemy uses. Never underestimate its ability to cloud your vision. Before we can truly grow in our faith and experience God's healing, we must first face and admit our denial.

> "Time is limited, so I better wake up every morning fresh and know that I have just one chance to live this particular day right and to string my days together into a life of action and purpose."
> –Lance Armstrong

The Mask of Pride

Dr. Gregory Jantz, author of *Hope, Help, and Healing for Eating Disorders* wrote,

> One of the prime factors in denial is that of pride. Pride encourages the denial of your eating disorder. If you are anorexic, you've got denial down pat—and you take an enormous amount of pride in the accomplishment of your weight loss. If you overeat, you may tell yourself that your behavior is normal due to your difficult circumstances—*I just need to feel better; and then I'll stop.* If you are a compulsive overeater, you are probably past the point of pretending that what you do is normal, but your pride may be keeping you from crying out for help.[11]

If you are bulimic, you believe you have enough willpower to just quit tomorrow. *Today's the last day.*

Some say we are all born with a mask of pride and selfishness. If so, my mask of pride morphed into a monster mask, and it wasn't easily discarded after Halloween. I learned that the pride I developed as a child had a motivating effect on the development of my abnormal eating patterns. It was a spiritual virus that infected my life.

Pride was blinding. As my eating patterns changed for the worst, pride told me that my behavior was acceptable and kept me from seeking help. Pride took center stage. *Look at what I have accomplished! I am in control! Look, I can squeeze into a size four.* In everything I did, I made certain that I got the credit. This was false self-confidence.

Pride is deceptive. We aspire to be number one because of self-importance and the need to be accepted. Instead of working toward our personal best (that *spirit of excellence*), we are determined to be better than everyone else (perfect). We take pride in the wrong things, don't we? Proverbs 27:2 says not to praise ourselves, but let others do it (if they only would!).

Have you read the book of Obadiah? Have you heard of the book of Obadiah? Obadiah had a message to us all. Historically, it's a message to the country of Edom (the country founded by Jacob's brother Esau, Genesis 25:30; 36:1).

Obadiah 1:1–4:

¹ This is what the Sovereign Lord says about Edom— We have heard a message from the Lord: An envoy was sent to the nations to say, "Rise, and let us go against her for battle"— ² "See, I will make you small among the nations; you will be utterly despised. ³ The pride of your heart has deceived you, you who live in the clefts of the rocks and make your home on the heights, you who say to yourself, 'Who can bring me down to the ground?' ⁴ Though you soar like the eagle and make your nest among the stars, from there I will bring you down," declares the Lord.

What is Obadiah's message to us? What principle can we learn from him?

Maybe you've earned that promotion, dropped down a dress size, got the coolest car, fixed your nose, or bought that home with a view (3). You may think you're soaring through life, feeling you have control over your food intake and everything else—you feel good enough to touch the stars (4). Obadiah reminds us that *we are not in control*—God is in control.

Reflective Questions

If you have a tendency to disobey God because you believe you know better, what one thing can you do differently this week to change that?

Is there pride in your heart? Whom is it against, and why? Write out your thoughts. Then write a prayer to God and repent of the pride you are harboring. *"Repent" simply means "turn around"—turn away from a life of sin and idolatry and turn towards the gracious love and will of God.*

Day Five: Other Masks of Pain

~

We've become pros at masking the pain.

My obsession with body image camouflaged the real person God created me to be, so I wore other masks to cover up my true feelings. Most of us don't realize or want to admit that the masks we wear are masks of sin.

The Mask of Jealousy and Envy

I always felt competitive with other women and had an uncontrollable lust for their possessions and position. Call me the "material girl." In high school, I became good friends with a cheerleader. Not only was she beautiful, smart, popular, dated the star of the football team, but she was wealthy and drove a sports car. *I'd give anything to be her! Why don't glamorous things happen to me?*

God knew envy was soul-destroying, so He prohibited it in the Ten Commandments: "Thou shall not covet . . ." To covet something is to long for, or envy, what someone else has. It may be material things or physical traits.

I began to realize I was comparing the *inside of me* to the *outside of her*. I was looking at her in her evening gown whilst standing there in my underwear. I found that if I took the time and examined her, her "inside" was just as disorderly, or more so, and then I was grateful for the blessings God had bestowed upon me.

Unbelievably, that cheerleader struggled with alcoholism and married four times.

Jealousy is Satan's lie. It wreaks havoc in our lives because we focus on earthly things and not on God. Jealousy hurts our relationship with others and more so our relationship with God. Proverbs 14:30 says, "A heart at peace gives life to the body, but envy rots the bones." That's spiritual osteoporosis!

Why not me? Pray for wisdom to accept your life as it is and to see the gifts and advantages you have today. Acceptance and gratitude are the antidotes to the soul-destroying poison of envy.

Reflective Questions

When were you wearing a mask of jealousy and envy?

Did you compare the inside of you to the outside of someone else? How?

The Mask of Judgment

I constantly compared myself to others. I'd go from *I'm fatter than you* to *I'm better than you.* Why not? Others judged me. Let's discard our mask of judgment!

The Bible tells us why we need to in Romans 2:1: "You, therefore, have no excuse, you who pass judgment on someone else, for at whatever point you judge the other, you are condemning yourself, because you who pass judgment do the same things."

Looking back, I realize just how much of my life has been spent dwelling upon the faults of others. It provided self-satisfaction, to be sure, but I see now just how subtle and actually perverse the process became. After all was said and done, the net effect of dwelling on the so-called faults of others was self-granted permission to remain comfortably unaware of my own defects.
—Anonymous

Paul provides some more good advice, "Finally, brothers, whatever is true, whatever is noble, whatever is right, whatever is pure, whatever is lovely, whatever is admirable—if anything is excellent or praiseworthy—think about such things" (Philippians 4:8).

We can usually find someone that we can outperform, underweigh, overdress, or outwit. But the one person we should compare ourselves to is Jesus Christ. We should ask ourselves two questions, (1) *Will I ever have to deny what I'm about to do?* and (2) *What would Jesus do or think in this situation?*

Reflective Questions

What are we to think about? What should we focus on in other people?

Which masks apply to you? What have you learned about yourself this week?

Finale: Week Two

~

Hope. It's an unbreakable spiritual lifeline.

Hope reaches past all appearances right to the very presence of God. Part of our healing is accepting the fact that we are not and will never be perfect. The masks of pain come from trying to be perfect. Perfection gets in the way of restoration because it imposes impossible, unrealistic goals that set us up for failure.

Jesus shows us that there is only one way to attain perfection—through Him. "Perfect" or "perfection" in biblical terms means fulfilling the purpose for which a person is made, not perfect in the sense of faultless. The perfection we receive from Him is not the same kind that the world seeks: physical perfection. Perfection is accepting and loving ourselves just as we are today.

If we don't think we have to be perfect, then we can accept our mistakes as learning experiences and be willing to try again. Say out loud: *I am thankful that I don't need to be perfect.*

What did you learn from this week's study that you can apply to your life this week?

Promise to Claim: "You have me endure many terrible troubles. You restore me to life again. You bring me back from the depths of the earth" (Psalm 71:20).

I Want More Bible Food!
Week Two: Pursuing Perfection God's Way

~

2 Corinthians 13:5–10

☑ In what ways does our culture reward personal beauty?

Paul wrote in his second letter to the church in Corinth, "Finally, brothers, good-bye. Aim for perfection, listen to my appeal, be of one mind, live in peace. And the God of love and peace will be with you" (2 Corinthians 13:11).

Read 2 Corinthians 13:5–10 to understand what Paul was referring to.

Do you think Paul was referring to the same kind of perfection we have been seeking, the physical perfection and achievement-oriented perfection? Why or why not?

_____

_____

_____

_____

_____

Week Three: Why Do I Hurt?

~

"Life is pain. The sharper, the more evidence of life."

We all have pain in our lives. Not necessarily illness, but deep, emotional pain caused by those who have hurt us. Loss causes pain, relationships cause pain, failure causes pain, and giving up on unrealistic goals causes pain. Don't we retreat at the first sign of trouble or misery? We've given up all hope of overcoming and learning from the experience. So we turn to food and substances to soothe the pain.

What can God do about it? *What can't God do?* is a better question. Our problems are so close to us and seem so much bigger than God. When life's problems loom over us, we tend to lose our sense of perspective, and God fades into the background. But in some mysterious way known only to God, we grow when our hearts are broken.

Suffering isn't pleasant but it's necessary. God doesn't *cause* our suffering but uses it. The enemy seems so busy in our matters that it's hard to trace the hand of God in it. But His hand is in it.

Did you know that pain broadens our base of experience and can make us stronger (or weaker)? The apostle Paul taught that suffering is an essential course in God's curriculum for all believers. "We must go through many hardships to enter the kingdom of God" (Acts 14:22). We become less judgmental, self-righteous, and less convinced that our way is right if we allow ourselves to express and feel pain. We become more compassionate in the end.

God wants believers to celebrate in their difficulties, to continue to put their hope and trust in Him, and grow stronger *in spite of* their experiences.

Day One: Discouraging Times

~

We live in depressing times.

Our world is tomorrow-oriented, and that can depress anyone. Proverbs 27:1 says, "Do not boast *(or fret)* about tomorrow, for you do not know what a day may bring forth." Let's focus on today.

You may wonder why God has left you in the situations you're in today. There is a reason for every victory and every defeat in your life. A reason for every mountain and every valley. A reason for every good day and every bad day.

King David is a good illustration. When David was in the cave (Psalm 142), he was hurting, and he shows us that today is very important. Psalms 142:1–7:

¹ I cry aloud to the Lord; I lift up my voice to the Lord for mercy. ² I pour out my complaint before him; before him I tell my trouble. ³ When my spirit grows faint within me, it is you who know my way. In the path where I walk men have hidden a snare for me. ⁴ Look to my right and see; no one is concerned for me. I have no refuge; no one cares for my life. ⁵ I cry to you, O Lord; I say, "You are my refuge, my portion in the land of the living." ⁶ Listen to my cry, for I am in desperate need; rescue me from those who pursue me, for they are too strong for me. ⁷ Set me free from my prison, that I may praise your name.

David is wondering how he could possibly live in this cave today. In verses 1, 5, and 6, he cries out to God. One of the reasons God loved David so much was because he cried so much. David also probably gave God a piece of his mind. *I was king. Now I'm in a cave. Why? Where are you, God?*

Every day, every moment, God had a reason for leaving David in the cave. David was learning a lesson too—to live for the moment. When you live for the moment, then you ask God, *What are you going to teach me today?* David discovers the willingness to live in the here and now, and he learns a wealth of different things.

In verse 2, David pours out everything before the Lord. In verse 6, he cries out for attention and asks for protection. His enemy is great, like the enemy we each face everyday. So what does he do? He asks for encouragement (7).

You may look at David's situation and think, *I'd be out of there!* It's so easy to run away from our problems and abandon all the pain, isn't it? Not David. He stays and cries out to the Lord. *I'm not quitting, no matter how long it takes you to work on me. I know when I get out of here, I'll be healed and a better person. Then my life will greatly affect others.*

This is a story of hope.

God knows the lessons we need to learn—lessons of patience, submission, and self-denial. Our faith may need strengthening. When we vent our heart to the Lord as David did, He uses our pain to draw us closer to Him. God can take you and raise you up like David. Someone once said that we humans have a tendency to crucify ourselves between two thieves: the regret of yesterday and the fear of tomorrow.

David prayed and told God how he felt. Let's not be so concerned about God getting us out of the cave that we miss the lessons He has for us. David wasn't in a hurry. We shouldn't be in a hurry either, because God's plans will make no sense. Like David, won't you pray? The Lord is waiting to hear from you.

Many times our prayers aren't answered immediately. The Bible tells us not to lose heart (Luke 18:1). Keep praying—don't cease. Sometimes God fulfills our desires. Sometimes He asks us to wait. Sometimes He turns down our requests so that He can give us something better. Often we're like that child who wants to play with a sharp knife. What does Mom do? She gives us something safer, something better to play with.

If God says no, then we must receive His will and move on. If He says yes, we praise Him for the answer. God honors persistent prayer, and it is not wrong to bring the same problem to Him over and over until you know His will.

If you feel like you're in that cave right now, make David's prayer your own. Praying is the greatest therapy I know. There is no listener like the Lord. He just sits and listens. Tell Him how you feel. Open the door and yell, cry, whatever you feel.

The Psalms say when you cry unto God, He stops everything and turns to you. He says, *How can I help you? What can I do?* He sets aside His time to listen to *you.* Because of God's unfailing love, trust that He has heard your prayer and answered it.

"God bestows favor and honor; *no good thing does he withhold* from those whose walk is blameless" (Psalm 84:11).

> "Yesterday is gone. Tomorrow has not yet come. We have only today. Let us begin."
>
> –Mother Teresa (1910–1997)

Reflective Questions

Victory comes to those who wait in the cave with God. How are you doing in your waiting?

What must you do today if you are going to walk in victory? How do you feel about your future?

Day Two: Why Do I Have to Suffer?

When we feel imprisoned, we ask, *Where is God?*

One night, Carol was purging for the third time in one hour. All of a sudden, she felt a piercing, stinging sensation in her throat and she began gagging. She looked down in the toilet bowl and witnessed a puddle of blood. *It's okay, she thought, I've bled before* (denial). But the blood kept coming. *What am I going to do? Who can I tell? Nobody knows my horrible, shameful secret.*

So she didn't tell anyone. For the next two days, Carol suffered and existed in agony. On the third day, she checked into the emergency room. *When I woke up, the doctor told me I had a very large ulcer in my throat that was on the verge of rupturing, which could lead to death.*

This is a picture of both physical and emotional suffering. We each have our own story. Why does this all-powerful God allow us to suffer so, especially if He is a loving God? The Bible doesn't spell out all of His reasons: "How impossible it is for us to understand his decisions and his methods!" (Romans 11:33, TLB). But the Bible does give us insights into how He uses troubles for good.

Peter goes so far as to insist that suffering is our calling. "To this you were called, *because Christ suffered for you,* leaving you an example, *that you should follow in his steps*" (1 Peter 2:22).

God has a specific objective in mind for our suffering. He knows exactly the intensity and the duration that's needed to fulfill His purposes. Through the whole process, whether it's days, weeks, months, or years, we have His promise. "The God of all grace, who called you to His eternal glory in Christ, after you have suffered a little while, will himself *restore you* and make you *strong, firm and steadfast*" (1 Peter 5:10). Oliver Wendell Holmes understood this truth when he wrote, "If I had a formula for ridding mankind of trouble, I think I would not reveal it, for in doing so, I would do him a disservice."[12]

Scripture doesn't say we won't pass through rough waters. What does God promise us in Isaiah 43:2? "When you pass through the waters, I will be with you; and when you pass through the rivers, they will not sweep over you. When you walk through the fire, you will not be burned; the flames will not set you ablaze."

God will be with us in those waters. It doesn't say that we won't have bad days. It doesn't tell us that rivers won't roar at our feet. Scripture tells us that *they will not overwhelm us.* There will be fiery places. But because of God's great love, we will not be consumed in the fire.

> "When life is good we tend to have no questions, but when life is bad we have no answers."
>
> —Mike Mason[13]

The Mystery Woman

Mark 5:25–43 speaks of a mystery woman in the crowd who had been slowly bleeding for twelve years. She had suffered a great deal and spent everything she had. She was desperate. She heard that Jesus was coming.

As the crowd gathered, she thought, *If I just touch his clothes, I will be healed.* (Notice she goes to Jesus; she does not wait around for Him to find her.) Jesus was near. She touched His robe. "Immediately her bleeding stopped and she felt in her body that she was freed from her suffering" (29).

Then Jesus asked, "Who touched me?" The woman stepped up. Trembling, she knelt before Him and told her story. No one listened before. But when this woman reached out to Jesus, He said, "Daughter, your faith has healed you. Go in peace and be freed from your suffering" (34).

These words represent hope! Jewish law considered her unclean, unsocial, and she must have been weak from anemia. She spent all her money on doctors but nothing worked. Jesus called her "daughter." This is the only time when Jesus calls a woman "daughter." He gave her a name when no one else did.

After her encounter with Jesus, I'm sure she overcame any feelings of inferiority and low self-esteem. I hope she realized that she, too, was created in the image of God, equal in value and giftedness, a precious daughter of the King. She, too, was royalty! A princess, just like you and me!

This story offers us encouragement. The hand that touched that woman can touch you. When Jesus walked this planet, He gave dignity and worth to every person. As we learn more about Jesus, we're reminded of His miraculous healing power to deal with prolonged sickness. *Henry David Thoreau said, "The smallest seed of faith is better than the largest fruit of happiness."*

What does her story tell you about faith? About claiming your identity? We can all count the ways we personally relate to her.

Reflective Questions

What insights from the bleeding woman story can you apply to your situation? In what ways can you personally relate to her? Think of as many examples as possible.

Based on what you have learned so far about God, what aspects of His character will you cling to in times of anguish?

Day Three: Silver and Gold

Suffering and glory go together.

You can't have one without the other. God equates our suffering to the purifying of silver and gold. Neither metal is pure in its natural state. Both are mixed with all sorts of gunk making them impure, just like us. Malachi 3:3 says, "He will sit as a refiner and purifier of silver; he will purify the Levites and refine them like gold and silver."

We are born with a sinful nature (as a result of the fall) that constantly attracts all sorts of impurities: thoughts, beliefs, destructive actions, and habits. We are influenced by a society permeated with sin. As silver and gold need to be refined before they reveal their beauty, so do we. The process of refining includes the melting down of the metal by fires designed not to destroy the metal, but bring forth its beauty.

The silver is crushed into small pieces and placed into a crucible. The silversmith places the crucible over the fire and then watches carefully as the silver melts. Eventually, impurities rise to the top of the crucible. The silversmith scrapes them off carefully. Then a hotter fire is built. Again, the silver is subjected to more heat. Under intense firing, more and different impurities are released.

The silversmith never leaves the silver unattended in the fire because too much heat may damage the silver. Each time the fire is amplified and impurities removed, the silversmith looks at himself in the melted silver.

At first, his image is dim. However, with each new fire his

image becomes clearer. When he visibly sees himself, he knows all the impurities are gone. The refining is complete!

So it is with us. God breaks us and puts us into the crucible of suffering for one purpose—to make us into His image. At first, large chunks of impurities surface, representing "big" sins, like stealing and lying. It's somewhat easy to skim these off. The process continues, and with each layer of impurities, the chunks get smaller and smaller. It takes longer to skim off the smaller impurities (representing unidentified sin and negative core beliefs) because they are harder to see.

If you are feeling the heat of the fire today, remember that God has His eye on you and will keep watching you until He sees His image in you and every tiny impurity is removed. Also remember, He is *not* the source of your pain. His Word says,

> ⁶*In this you greatly rejoice, though now for a little while you may have had to suffer grief in all kinds of trials.*
> ⁷ *These have come so that your faith—of greater worth than gold, which perishes even though refined by fire—may be proved genuine and may result in praise, glory and honor when Jesus Christ is revealed.*
> ⁸ *Though you have not seen him, you love him; and even though you do not see him now, you believe in him and are filled with an inexpressible and glorious joy (1 Peter 1:6–8).*

Don't be afraid. God is ever present. God has been there through every trial, pain, and hurt. He's had His hand on each situation so that it wouldn't destroy us, knowing that eventually it would work together for good. This gives us courage as we walk through the turmoil.

Learn to see every trial, past, present, and future, as part of God's refining process to make you more like Jesus, because with each trial, we are called upon to make a decision. *To avoid the trials forces us to reject the lessons God wants to teach us.* Will you believe God and respond in the way He says to respond?

2 Timothy 2:12 says, "If we endure, we will also reign with

him. If we disown him, he will also disown us." If we do *not* respond to the truth of God's Word and allow it to transform us into His image, then God can do nothing more with us.

> "The gem cannot be polished without friction, nor man perfected without trials."
>
> –Chinese Proverb

Reflective Questions

Come to God now and talk to Him about a struggle you are experiencing. How do you want to respond to this struggle?

Can you trust God when you don't understand? Give your thoughts to God and pray for help to understand. Then wait as He turns your struggle into triumph.

Day Four: Divine Pruning

~

A beautiful, healthy garden requires pruning.

The dictionary[14] says to prune is (1) to cut off or remove dead or living parts or branches to improve shape or growth, and (2) to remove what is unnecessary or undesirable. God does this with us. Sometimes we suffer because God is "pruning" us. What do these verses tell us about our garden and about us?

In, John 15:1–5, Jesus said:

¹ *"I am the true vine, and my Father is the gardener.*

² He cuts off every branch in me that bears no fruit, while every branch that does bear fruit he prunes so that it will be even more fruitful.

³ You are already clean because of the word I have spoken to you.

⁴ Remain in me, and I will remain in you. No branch can bear fruit by itself; it must remain in the vine. Neither can you bear fruit unless you remain in me.

⁵ "I am the vine; you are the branches. *If a man remains in me and I in him, he will bear much fruit; apart from me you can do nothing."*

What if I told you that you needed to endure a long, intense, and difficult trial so that God could prune away some of the sin in your life? What if that trial leads to a healthier you?

We all have felt pruned at one time. Perhaps it was when your father left home and divorced your mother, or when you were passed over for that job or promotion. Pruning is painful but profitable. James tells us that trials are occasions for joy because they will test our faith and *develop in us perseverance and maturity* (character). We need God's help even to desire to yield ourselves to His pruning, don't we?

"I am the vine; you are the branches. If a man remains in me and I in him, he will bear much fruit; apart from me you can do nothing" (5). What a beautiful description of our personal relationship with Christ. We abide in Him and He in us. We are part of Him, rooted and grounded in Him.

> "Though he slay me, yet will I trust in him. If he wounds it is to heal . . . He would not thus prune the tree if he had sentenced it to be cut down."
>
> –William Jay

The Development of Character

Romans 5:3–5:

Not only so, but we also rejoice in our sufferings, because we know that suffering produces perseverance; perseverance, character; and character, hope. And hope does not disappoint us, because God has poured out his love into our hearts by the Holy Spirit, whom he has given us.

Paul says that we should respond to life's trials by rejoicing in our sufferings. *Rejoice? Why would he say that?* Paul said, "Because we know that suffering produces perseverance." He tells us that as believers, we rejoice in our suffering because of what we *know* about suffering.

When we go through a particular trial, we should ask if God's intention:

• Is corrective? Psalm 119:67: "Before I was afflicted I went astray, but now I obey your word."

• Is routine? Job 5:7: "Mankind heads for sin and misery as predictably as flames shoot upwards from a fire" (TLB).

• Is designed to glorify Jesus? John 9:3: "Neither this man nor his parents sinned," said Jesus, "but this happened so that the work of God might be displayed in his life."

Paul is telling us how God develops our character through our suffering:

- Suffering produces perseverance.
- Suffering produces character.
- Suffering produces hope.

No trial comes except by His permission for some wise and loving purpose. God doesn't owe us an explanation, and He may choose not to disclose the "why" until we meet Him in eternity. We need to trust Him even when we don't understand. That trust is independent of understanding.

Putting our trust in God is like being awake during surgery. He is not finished with us; He is still creating us, making us just as He has been all along from the beginning. For the short span of our life on earth, we have the extraordinary privilege of being wide-awake as God continues to mold and fashion us. We can watch His fingers at work within our heart and spirit.

This can be a painful process, and there is no anesthesia. The only anesthesia is trust—trust in the Surgeon. God *is* in complete control.

Reflective Questions

When we do things our way and not God's way, what are we really doing?

Why should you rejoice in your suffering even when you don't know the reason? How can you do this?

Day Five: Calvary's Love

~

It's been paid for.

I was sitting in a restaurant, eating my dinner, when a wino came in and ordered a sandwich. When the waiter gave him the check and asked him to pay, he said he didn't have the money. The waiter was infuriated because he'd have to pay for the wino's sandwich. He got so mad he started beating him up. One patron yelled, "Leave him alone! I'll pay for his sandwich." The wino dragged himself up and said, "Keep your money, you don't have to pay. I just did." At that moment, I witnessed "the blood of the cross."

–Anonymous

The wino paid with his bruises and blood. Our beloved Savior, Jesus, paid with His life. He submitted to the scourging (whipping, flogging, lashes, beatings, bruises) of His tormentors. Jesus paid for us the way the wino paid for his sandwich with bruises and blood. As Jesus hung nailed to that cross, and as He looks at the mess we've created in our lives, He says, "You don't have to pay, I already did."

"A minister was told by a person he helped, 'You are a good man.' He replied, 'I'm not a good man. I am sinful, selfish, and sick; Jesus Christ has laid his hands on me, that's all.'"

–A. Philip Parham[15]

The Secret to Healing

There are no easy answers to suffering. We hear, *Get a grip.* The only way to get a grip is through the cross. What does the cross really mean?

The answer, in part, is that the cross never promises to free us from pain and suffering. In fact, the cross promises just the opposite; it promises certainty of pain and suffering. You say, *I don't want it then!* Listen on. If we are going to learn to deal with our suffering and hurts God's way, then we must come to know that Jesus is our refuge.

When Christ left heaven for earth, He became a faithful High Priest who completely understands our human condition. Jesus was often hungry, tired, and thirsty. He was tempted and betrayed. "For we do not have a high priest who is unable to sympathize with our weaknesses, but we have one who has been tempted in every way, just as we are—yet was without sin" (Hebrews 4:15). *He knows how we feel.*

When Jesus walked among us, He healed the sick and the demon-possessed. When He went to Calvary, He healed all of us—all of our sins—through His death on the cross. It is important to focus on the Healer, not the healing. Can you comprehend that?

"Surely he took up our infirmities (*our grief, our pain*) and carried our sorrows (*sickness, disorder*), yet we considered him stricken by God, smitten by him, and afflicted" (Isaiah 53:4).

The Cross Heals

The reason God became man in the person of Jesus was to die for our sins. Sin wounds, the cross heals! The cross is the place God has chosen for us to come to Him in humble faith and obedience, in opposition to our pride, in order to be forgiven, and ultimately delivered from the punishment we rightly deserve.

Isaiah 53:5–6:

⁵ *But he was pierced for our transgressions* (violation of a law or a duty or moral principle), *he was crushed for our iniquities* (immoral act; a sin)*; the punishment that brought us peace was upon him, and by his wounds we are healed.*⁶ *We all, like sheep, have gone astray, each of us has turned to his own way; and the Lord has laid on him*(self) *the iniquity*(sin) *of us all.*

"By his wounds we are healed." Healed of what? Scripture can help us interpret scripture.

1 Peter 2:24–25:
²⁴ *He himself bore our sins in his body on the tree, so that we might die to sins and live for righteousness; by his wounds you have been healed.*²⁵ *For you were like sheep going astray, but now you have returned to the Shepherd and Overseer of your souls.*

According to both these passages, the cross was God's means of saving us from sin so that we could live righteous lives (the opposite of sin is righteous). Our slates have been wiped clean. The real healing our body needs is forgiveness of our sins. *Those shameful and destructive secrets have been nailed to Christ's cross.* That's a real body makeover!

By God's grace we can put away all our painful masks. Colossians 3:1–5 gives us the key to freedom:

¹ *Since, then, you have been raised with Christ, set your hearts on things above, where Christ is seated at the right hand of God.*² *Set your minds on things above, not on earthly things.*³ *For you died, and your life is now hidden with Christ in God.* ⁴ *When Christ, who is your life, appears, then you also will appear with him in glory.* ⁵ *Put to death, therefore, whatever belongs to your earthly nature: sexual immorality, impurity, lust, evil desires and greed, which is idolatry.*

No matter what's happened in our past, we can live *without* possessiveness, anger, hate, bitterness, jealousy, and envy. We can live a life free from perfection, free from that which causes distortment of our body image (and ultimately destruction). The starting point is setting our hearts and minds on the things above.

The Reward

We must intentionally focus on Jesus Christ and continually remind ourselves that because of His death on the cross, *we are forgiven of every sinful act and desire and are no longer enslaved by sin.* Once we accept Jesus Christ as our personal Savior, confess (means to tell God, bring out into the open) our sins, God *does not see* our past anymore (it's completely erased). *He gets very excited for our future!*

Each one of us has been searching for the secret to healing and restoration. This is it! *You have just unlocked the mystery behind returning to a normal life.*

This is a free gift! You're already in—it's not through some secretive initiation or application process but rather through what Christ has already done for you at Calvary.

God has raised you from the dead as He did Christ. When you were stuck in your old sin-dead life, you were incapable of responding to God. *God has now brought you back to life.* Jesus' work as far as our salvation is complete. When He hung on the cross, He said, "It is finished" (John 19:30).

> "Jesus didn't come just to rescue us from hell; He came to rescue us from a life of hell on earth."
>
> –Sheila Walsh[16]

Reflective Questions

Do you think Jesus can really empathize with your situation? Why or why not?

How does Jesus' work on Calvary (the cross) provide for your healing?

Finale: Week Three

~

Jesus understands every weakness of ours.

Jesus was tempted in every way we are, but He did not sin. So whenever we are in need, we should come bravely before the throne of God. "Let us then approach the throne of grace with confidence, so that we may receive mercy and find grace to help us in our time of need" (Hebrews 4:16). Jesus wants us to know that in the times of our darkness, we can be safe in Him.

We might think seriously about these words of Socrates, especially if we compare ourselves to others and want to trade our lives: "If all our misfortunes were laid in one common heap whence everyone must take an equal portion, most people would be content to take their own and depart."

We should remember that the problems before us are *never* bigger than the Power behind us. Regardless of how dark it seems right now, there is an end in sight!

"When the earth and all its people quake, it is I who hold its pillars firm" (Psalms 75:3).

What did you learn from this week's study that you can apply to your life?

> Promise to Claim: "Heal me, O Lord, and I will be healed; save me and I will be saved, for you are the one I praise"
> (Jeremiah 17:14).

I Want More Bible Food!
Week Three: Why Do I Hurt?

~

Mark 5:21–43

☑ Have you ever felt that God treated you unfairly, that He owed you an explanation for why you were suffering? Explain.

As we learn more about Jesus, we're reminded of His miraculous healing power to deal with prolonged sickness.

Read Mark 5:21–34: The Dead Girl and Mystery (Sick) Woman

Read verses 21–24. What do we learn about the crowd? About Jairus, a synagogue ruler? List as many insights as you can find.

_____

_____

_____

_____

_____

What insights do you observe about Jesus from verses 23–24?

_____

_____

_____

How can you apply this to your life and those close to you?
Share an example.

_____

_____

_____

_____

_____

Read verses 25–34. What were the specifics of this bleeding woman's situation? Who did she look to for healing?

_____

_____

_____

_____

_____

This story offers us hope. How do these verses provide further encouragement?

Matthew 17:20

_____

Mark 11:24

_____

Romans 5:1

_____

Ephesians 2:8

_____

How has your faith been strengthened from these promises?

_____

_____

_____

Read Mark 5:35–43.

What were the specifics of the situation with the little girl? How did Jesus handle the situation?

_____

_____

_____

Is there a present situation where you need Jesus to do the same?

_____

_____

_____

What comparisons or contrasts do you see between the bleeding woman and the dead girl? Use the chart to answer.

The Bleeding Woman	Comparisons or Contrasts	The Dead Girl

How does this compare to what Jairus and the bleeding woman did?

_____

_____

_____

In today's society, how might we (man) go about seeking relief or healing? What will you do differently the next time you seek help?

_____

_____

_____

_____

_____

☑ Whatever problems you have, none are too silly or personal to take to Jesus. He might offer you instant healing or inspiration to try something entirely different. What is one way you can use what you have learned about faith and healing to change your life this week?

Week Four: Seeking the Truth

Why are we so unhappy with our bodies?

In Week Two, we learned that we are under pressure to measure up to a certain social and cultural ideal of beauty, which can lead to poor body image. Images we see daily can reinforce an already negative opinion we have of our body, leading us to believe we are overweight and not able to meet the "perfect" American standard.

Family and friends can influence our body image with positive and/or negative comments. Doctors and other professionals also have a powerful impact on our body image. Their comments may be delivered as health advice, but if misinterpreted, affects how we perceive our body.

We all have days when we feel awkward or uncomfortable in our bodies. The key to developing positive body image is to recognize and respect our natural shape and learn to overpower those negative thoughts and feelings with positive, affirming, and accepting thoughts.

Accept yourself. Accept your body. Celebrate yourself. Celebrate your body. Let's get going!

Day One: Body Image and Self-Esteem

~

What is body image?

Slowly over time, you developed your body image based on what your family, boyfriend(s), and/or husband(s), coaches, and teachers told you. Add to that thousands of daily media messages from magazines, novels, television, music, and *you start to believe* that you're fat or ugly. All these negative thoughts and beliefs can lead down a self-destructive path unless you know how to recognize and cope with them.

Dr. Deborah Newman, author of *Loving Your Body,* says a woman with a healthy body image respects her body, takes care of her body, and keeps her body in perspective.[17]

What is self-esteem?

Self-esteem is defined as "a confidence and satisfaction in oneself." It is your overall evaluation of your self-worth and how you value your own attributes. How high or low your self-esteem is depends on how you compare what you'd like to be with how you actually see yourself.

Research shows that girls lose twenty-three percent of their self-esteem between elementary and middle school. A study by the American Association of University Women found only twenty-nine percent of high school girls were happy with themselves.[18]

Psychologists describe key components of self-esteem as how you evaluate yourself in terms of important characteristics like what you are good at, what you are not so good at, and the kinds of situations you prefer or avoid.

Most of our feelings about ourselves are built into us in childhood. If we were fortunate to have loving parents who conveyed our worth in their relationship to us, and if we grew up in a safe environment with positive relationships with peers, teachers, and role models, then it is likely we will feel reasonably good about ourselves. However, if faced with negative influences in childhood, it may not take much to tip the balance the other way.

> "The body is a sacred garment. It's your first and last garment; it is what you enter life in and what you depart life with, and it should be treated with honor."
>
> –Martha Graham[19]

Real Beauty Comes From the Potter

Genuine beauty is a rare quality that very few find because it doesn't come easily or is even natural. Real beauty takes refinement like the silver we talked about. Only a submitted life can be a life of beauty. I asked God to help me overcome my attitude (obsession) about beauty, and He pointed me to the potter and the clay.

Jeremiah 18:1–6:

[1] *This is the word that came to Jeremiah from the Lord:* [2] *"Go down to the potter's house, and there I will give you my message."* [3] *So I went down to the potter's house, and I saw him working at the wheel.* [4] *But the pot he was shaping from the clay was marred in his hands; so the potter formed it into another pot, shaping it as seemed best to him.* [5] *Then the word of the Lord came to me:* [6] *"O house of Israel, can I not do with you as this potter does?" declares the Lord. "Like clay in the hand of the potter, so are you in my hand, O house of Israel."*

The potter's wheel turns around and around. His gentle fingers form soft clay into a special creation. To this potter, there is a purpose in each turn.

God is the potter. The potter has power over the clay, and that power is unlimited. The clay on the potter's wheel can't talk back. It is helpless and hopeless. The clay can *only yield to the potter's hand.*

Who is the clay? We are the clay.

But *together,* the potter and the clay create works of art, objects of beauty. These objects of beauty were at one time on the potter's wheel, a shapeless mass of mud. Then the clay yielded to the potter's hand. As the lifeless clay lay under the hand of the potter, He molded and made the clay into beautiful clay jars (or vessels).

The Clay Jars

The potter wants to use clay. He wants something that He can put in His hand to mold and fashion. God wants to work with you and me. He has a purpose. He's not just playing around like a child with play-doh. *This is God's work, and He knows what He is doing.*

Paul tells us in 2 Corinthians 4:5–9 that our light, our knowledge, our power comes from God, not from within us. God shows us His glory as the "treasure" in the clay jar.

We have been obsessed with taking care of the outside of the clay jar. We've meticulously tried to cover the cracks with food, alcohol, and/or pills. We'll preserve the clay jar at any cost, won't we?

Right now you may be feeling more as if your life is broken pottery (cracked pots, not crackpot), spewed in tiny pieces all over the floor.

If I am the clay on the Potter's wheel, should I tell God that I don't like my body? My appearance? No, God has a purpose for my life and that comforts me. While I don't know my specific purpose, I know I can trust Him to mold me into His special clay jar filled with His treasure. That's real beauty.

Lord, you are the Potter of my life. Let me surrender to Your molding so I can be a clay jar full of Your treasure and able to follow Your perfect plan.

Reflective Questions

How do you see yourself when you look in the mirror or when you picture yourself in your mind?

What do you believe about your own appearance (including your memories, assumptions, and generalizations)?

How do you feel about your body, including your height, shape, and weight?

How do you feel *in* your body, not just *about* your body.

Day Two: Searching for Your True Identity?

~

Mirror, mirror on the wall, who is the fairest of them all?

Fat, ugly, unloved, wrinkled, and worthless. This is often what we think as we look in the mirror. There are days when we feel ugly no matter how much time we put into looking good. Some days we feel like mistakes dressing up as people.

Criticizing ourselves on the outside is usually caused by the way we feel inside. When we measure ourselves by our physical appearance, we will always feel let down. *No one can always be the fairest of them all.*

Everyone wants to feel attractive and loved. The problem is that the more we focus on what we look like on the outside, the less fulfillment and joy comes from the inside. I know. I've tried it. My search railroaded me off God's super-highway onto an empty, unfulfilling gravel road filled with potholes. I was blinded to the beauty God had planned for my life.

Slowly we are beginning to understand how our real glow comes from the inside. We are meeting people who aren't beauty contest winners on the outside but who shine because of their personalities, positive energy, and Jesus. An old Danish proverb goes, "What you are is God's gift to you. What you do with yourself is your gift to God."

☑ God gave each one of us gifts and talents, but we've buried them under our issues and habits. Take some time to think about the gifts and talents God gave you. Gifts are the things you were born doing well, while talents are those things you must practice doing. Over the week, pray and ask God to open your eyes to the gifts and talents He gave you, then write them down in your journal.

My Self-Worth

Did you know that your birth was not a mistake? Your parents may not have planned to have you, *but God planned your birth. He welcomed your birth.* Long before your parents conceived you, God conceived you. He thought of you first. *You are alive because God wanted to create you!*

Ephesians 1:4–5; 11 tells us about our birth: "For *he chose us* in him before the creation of the world to be holy and blameless in his sight. In love *he predestined us* to be adopted as his sons through Jesus Christ, in accordance with his pleasure and will."

God specializes in giving people like us a fresh start! The past is past. Nothing can change that. **We don't want to live in the past, but we can learn to live comfortably with it.** Wonderful changes are going to happen in your life as you begin to live it with God. How do we know that? "For I know the plans I have for you," declares the Lord, "plans to prosper you and not to harm you, plans to give you hope and a future" (Jeremiah 29:11). *Lord, today let me accept myself as a beautiful person inside and out. I make mistakes, but I am not a mistake!*

☑ Fill in these blanks or write out your own prayer:

Dear God, I'm just discovering that I'm beautiful and loved because You made me this way. Sometimes it's hard for me to believe that because _____. I have a hard time thinking of my_____ as beautiful. And that's because _____ . Lord, please help me to deal with _____ , and most of all help me to remember that you love me, that You made me perfect, that I can have God-confidence that makes me so unique. In Jesus' name, Amen.

Day Three: Conquering Fear

~

Feel is immobilizing.

Someone once said that courage is fear that has said its prayers.

Jessica wrote, "Fear has permeated every part of my life. Fear of being punished by God for what I've done and for not letting Him into my life. Fear for my health. Fear of losing my job. Fear that what I believe about myself is true. Fear that my children will grow up and resent me. Fear that my marriage will fail. Fear that people will learn the ugly truth about me. Fear that I will never get better because I am beyond repair. Fear that this pain will never end. Fear that my life will come to a tragic end."

What Am I Afraid Of?

Change, God, gaining weight, losing weight, relapsing, not being perfect, disapproval, therapy, medication, a strict new regime, being judged, restoring broken relationships, or a whole new lifestyle? Some say they are not even sure they would know how to live if they were healed. What happens to us if we let fear control us?

1. Fear immobilizes.
2. Fear opens the door for the work of Satan (leading to sin).
3. Fear causes physical problems.
4. Fear brings confusion and isolation.
5. Fear causes us to abandon relationships and love for others.
6. Fear keeps us from knowing and serving God.

A big component of the pain we feel is fear. Fear that this

disorder may never go away, like an unmoving cloud cover. In the midst of the pain and fear, we can acknowledge it and give it to God. Fear isn't a life sentence!

Almost every book in the Bible has a "fear not" verse in it. The enemy uses fear, but God asks us to have faith in Him. *Fear is always the enemy of faith.* Jesus challenges us to have faith to conquer fear (Matthew 21:21–22). *God's love for us and our faith in God will remove our fear.*

The Bible lists many failures and fears of spiritual leaders to show the grace and strength of God, *not people.* "The Lord is my light and my salvation. Who is there to fear? The Lord is my life's fortress. Who is there to be afraid of?" (Psalm 27:1)

I think this is one of the most powerful verses in the Bible. Isaiah 52:12 says, "But you will not leave in haste or go in flight; for the Lord will go before you, the God of Israel will be your rear guard."

Isaiah is saying that God has you *completely covered.* If that is the case, and we know His Word is truth, then *what is there to fear?*

"I am not afraid of storms, for I am learning how to sail my ship."

—Louisa May Alcott (1832–1888)

Change is Necessary

Fear of change, unwillingness to change, and lack of confidence in our ability to change are all roadblocks to healing. Our resistance to change may simply be the fear of trying something new, like a new eating plan. While we view this change as risky, it is necessary for healthy restoration.

I was afraid to try a new food plan for fear I would gain weight and fail at working it. Let's start by simply accepting the idea that change is sometimes necessary. After that, we can expect God to guide us into new situations that are right for us. God's answer to fear and discouragement is the assurance of His never-failing presence.

In the book of Exodus, God had been with Moses in a mighty way. Then Joshua took his place. Those were big footsteps to follow. God told Joshua that no matter where he went, what he experienced, He would be with him. He would never leave him. "Have I not commanded you? Be strong and courageous. Do not be terrified; do not be discouraged, for the Lord your God will be with you wherever you go" (Joshua 1:9).

Fear is a very uncomfortable emotion. When God says, "Do not fear," it is not a command of authority, but rather a word of comfort—a specific promise of God's presence with us. God *comforts* us just as our parents comforted us when we were frightened of the dark.

God offers us strength because He knows how fear torments us. If we are afraid and not trusting God, the only other option is to trust ourselves or trust another person (which usually doesn't work). David said, "In God I trust; I will not be afraid. What can man do to me?" (Psalm 56:11). He reassures us by saying that God puts His angels in charge of us to protect us in all our ways (Psalm 91:11).

Reflective Questions

List your greatest fears. Pray and ask God to make you aware of fears you may be ignoring.

What is your plan to overcome your fear(s)? Come back to your list and plan this week and continue to pray about your fears.

Day Four: Lies Versus Truths

Truth is like surgery—it may hurt, but it heals.

What is truth? "God's Word is truth" (John 17:17). Truth is powerful. John 8:32 says, "Then you will know the truth, and the truth will set you free." Truth is available to anyone who seeks it in Jesus Christ. Jesus said, "I am the way and *the truth* and the life" (John 14:6).

What is a lie? A false statement deliberately presented as being true; a falsehood; something meant to deceive or give a wrong impression[20] Denial is a lie.

How We Become Entrapped

My Dear Followers,

The following instructions shall help you handicap female believers and convince them to come on our side. One of our greatest allies at present is her perception of herself. It is your task, therefore, to feed her poor self-esteem. Already she wastes time primping in front of the mirror and worrying about her looks.

You must continue to encourage her to compare herself to those whom she admires. This will eventually immobilize her. When she feels inadequate, she will no longer attempt anything for Christ's kingdom because of her fear of failure. Her warped self-image will lead to unhealthy relationships and hinder her ability to love others. The more often she tells herself that she is a bad person and not competent, the more easily she will feel threatened by others. This will turn others off to Christ and his loathsome Christianity.

Finally, emphasize her weaknesses so that she begins to believe that she is unimportant to Christ. This will push her to compulsive striving to please him through her own accomplishments. Her works will no longer be motivated by faith, but by a dislike for herself. Confuse her so that she never feels forgiven. If you successfully convince her that Christ is never pleased with her, she will grow weary and give up altogether. [21]

This is what Satan does to us. He gets us to hate ourselves, become embittered to others, and blame those who are important to us. He uses other people's remarks to hurt us or create fear in our heart. This happens because we never were told the truth. The truth is, "Your enemy the devil prowls around like a roaring lion looking for someone to devour" (1 Peter 5:8). And "he is a thief that comes only to steal and kill and destroy" (John 10:10).

Few of us consider the consequences of our choices. Look at me. I saw beautiful, thin women being paraded around telling me this is what I had to look like. Because my body and beauty weren't naturally like a super-model, I made some bad choices trying to attain that look. At the time, these choices seemed acceptable. I felt good when people complimented me. I was innocent. But I ended up trapped for nearly twenty years. *I was deceived!* I cared more about looking like a model than pleasing my Father, my Creator.

How Did This All Start?

Satan's lie was the starting place for all the trouble in this world. It starts with the story of Adam and Eve. Satan's objective was to drive a wedge between God and His children, Adam and Eve. He knew they would not go against God, so he subtly tricked them with a reasonable and desirable offer.

Satan deceived Eve through a clever combination of outright lies disguised as truth. He began by planting seeds of doubt in her mind and by suggesting that God had said something that He had not said. Satan further deceived Eve by causing her to question the love and motives of God. Did God really say, "You must not eat from any tree in the garden?" (Genesis 3:1) He basically says,

That's a lie! You won't die! God knows very well that the instant you eat it, you will become like him! What an offer!

The truth is that God had said they were free to eat from any tree in the garden except one. "Do not eat from the Tree of the Knowledge of Good and Evil." God said, "When you eat of it you will surely die" (Genesis 2:17), Satan countered with, "You will not surely die . . . For God knows that when you eat of it your eyes will be opened, and you will be like God, knowing good and evil" (Genesis 3:4–5). He basically says, *That's a lie! You won't die! God knows very well that the instant you eat it, you will become like him!* What an offer! For the first time in history, a lie was spoken (and Eve did die).

"Then the Lord God said to the woman, 'What is this you have done?' The woman said, 'The serpent deceived me, and I ate'" (13). Eve then recognized she was deceived. From that moment to today, Satan has used deception to win our love, influence our choices, and destroy our lives. Satan uses similar reasoning with us as he tempts us to water down God's word. He tells us to make our own choices, choices that appear sensible. Instead of asking, "God, did you really say?" we think we know what we need, and so we move forward on our own and state, "God did not really say."

Why Do We Fall for His Deception?

Satan doesn't appear in the form of a serpent today. Often he comes as a romance novel, magazine, movie, soap opera, advertisement, or a song. He may also pose as someone giving sincere counsel. Anytime we receive input that is not consistent with the Word of God, we can be sure Satan is trying to deceive us. *What we read or hear may sound, feel, and seem right, but if it is contrary to the Word of God, it isn't right.*

Romans 1:25 tells us why we fall in the deception trap: "They exchanged the truth of God for a lie, and worshiped and served created things (idols) rather than the Creator."

How Do We Come to Think Like This?

- First, Satan plants the lie.
- Next, *we listen to the lie* and then dwell on it.
- We *begin to follow* what Satan has placed in our mind.
- We contemplate that this feels or sounds right, so *we believe the lie.*
- We rationalize it then consent and *act on the lie.*

Our beliefs get stronger that produce behavior, which in our case is destructive, sinful behavior. And sin always affects others, just as it did with Adam and Eve.

The Bible tells of God's effort to restore the fallen spirit. He worked with Adam and Eve, and later Noah and Abraham's family. He was their parent and passionately pursued them with love. The Bible always shows God trying to break through to human beings *in order to restore what had been lost.* He's trying to do the same with us today.

Reflective Questions

Have you allowed God to be truth in your life? Why or why not? How will you allow Him to be truth? Write the process out.

Satan knows that you will be more vulnerable to deception if you are not regularly meditating on God's Word. What step will you take to make God foremost in all your thoughts? Think of the things that will keep you away from consistent study of the Word. What can you do to change that?

Day Five: Who Am I?

~

Every act of sin begins with a lie.

And we don't just sin once, but over and over again. It's human nature. Before we know it, we're in bondage to food. Satan threw out the food bait, we took it, and he reeled us in. We didn't see the hook. He convinced us that his ideas were the right ones.

Think of it this way. Your mind is like a computer. In your computer, you've probably got years of data collected. In your mind, you have years of rejection, hurt, deception, and anger programmed. You made a choice: to believe the data or not; to delete the data or not.

"Truth is nowhere to be found, and whoever shuns evil becomes a prey. The Lord looked and was displeased that there was no justice" (Isaiah 59:15).

The word "truth" appears more than 224 times in the Bible. We need to begin to deal with the lies that put us in bondage and replace them with the truth. The truth will set us free. By giving ourselves to Jesus, we begin to see Satan's power and lies, then we begin to resist him. Dr. Larry Crabb said, "The soul will not be healed without truth."[22]

It has been said that Satan trembles when he sees the weakest saint upon his knees. That's not because he is afraid of us. It's because he knows that the power of God gives us victory over the works of darkness.

Praise God with Prayer

☑ When was the last time that you praised God for the way He created you? Anything less than a heart filled with gratitude and praise to God for our appearance grieves the Lord and is considered sinful. Write a prayer about the things you want to remember about being uniquely you.

Speak It Out: The Truth Will Set Me Free!

2 Corinthians 10:5 says we are to take captive every thought and make it obedient to Christ. If God can say these things about you, then you can say these things about yourself. Start by reminding yourself *you are a child of the Almighty God.* Truth!

We have to battle directly the enemy's lies and confusion. The antidote for deception is truth. As you recognize a lie, defend yourself out loud. Those that meditate over and speak God's Word's out loud tend to change their thinking and habits faster. *Truth changes our thinking, and thinking changes our behavior.* Achieving a new way of life consists of repeating positive actions.

☑ Read the following list and find the statements that best describe you. Then *speak it out* loud in your own words from your heart!

Corrupt Data: I am fat.

Speak it out: I am beautiful! I am fearfully and wonderfully made!

God's Word: Psalms 139:14; 1 Peter 3:3–4

Corrupt Data: I am dumb and stupid.

Speak it out: I have the mind of Christ!

God's Word: 1 Corinthians 2:16

Corrupt Data: I can't! I've been sick too long and I can't get well.

Speak it out: I can do all things through Christ who strengthens me!
God's Word: Philippians 4:13

Corrupt Data: I am ugly.
Speak it out: I am made in God's image!
God's Word: Genesis 1:27

Corrupt Data: Nothing I've tried works. I am weak and a lost cause.
Speak it out: I am strong!
God's Word: 2 Corinthians 12:9; Joel 3:10

Corrupt Data: I am lost. I don't know how to get back to normal.
Speak it out: I am found!
God's Word: Psalm 23:1–4; Luke 15:6

Corrupt Data: I am a victim of my past and will never be able to overcome that.
Speak it out: I am a victor!
God's Word: Psalm 60:12; 1 Corinthians 15:57

Corrupt Data: I am nothing. I am worthless.
Speak it out: I am treasured!
God's Word: Deuteronomy 7:6

Corrupt Data: I am so scared.
Speak it out: I am safe!
God's Word: Proverbs 18:10; Psalms 3:3

Corrupt Data: I can never be healed. I don't deserve to be healed.
Speak it out: I am healed!
God's Word: Isaiah 53:5

Corrupt Data: I am not loved.
Speak it out: God loves me!
God's Word: John 15:9

Corrupt Data: I have been addicted to food for over "x" years. I'll never be free.
Speak it out: The Spirit lives in me—I am free!
God's Word: 2 Corinthians 3:17

Corrupt Data: No one likes me. You wouldn't like me.
Speak it out: My worth is in who God says I am!
God's Word: Psalms 8:5–8

These are God's Words. So get into His Word (the Bible) everyday. Not only will you begin to see the truth, but also your faith will grow stronger. You will find that over time, your spiritual muscles of resisting Satan will grow, and the battle will get easier.

Speak it out: I am beautiful! I am lovable! I am worthy. I am capable! I'm not just saying that—God says that!

Reflective Question

What frequent negative thoughts do you have about yourself and your body? Now challenge each of these thoughts from the truth list.

Finale: Week Four

~

22 Do not merely listen to the word, and so deceive yourselves. Do what it says. 23 Anyone who listens to the word but does not do what it says is like a man who looks at his face in a mirror 24 and, after looking at himself, goes away and immediately forgets what he looks like. 25 But the man who looks intently into the perfect law that gives freedom, and continues to do this, not forgetting what he has heard, but doing it—he will be blessed in what he does.

James 1:22–25 is a very powerful, *truthful* verse. There are three roads to travel in life: the way of self, the way of Satan, and the way of God. The way of Satan and the way of self see us merely as a body or a face, and teach us that our value comes from our appearance or ability to perform. God's way tells us that we were uniquely created by a loving God who continually offers loving forgiveness. He offers the life-changing power of grace.

Lord, please clip my wings just a little to keep me nearer to You, to learn and be content with my limitations. Let me put Your will first in my life, not the will of others. Give me strength to say no in a loving but firm way. Help me not to be afraid or feel guilty. Help me to mend and absorb Your healing strength.

We have a choice as to which road we will take. Which road will you take?

Promise to Claim: "If you hold to my teaching, you are really my disciples. Then you will know the truth, and the truth will set you free" (John 8:31–32).

I Want More Bible Food!
Week Four: Seeking the Truth

~

Ezekiel 16:4–19

☑ Would you say you have low, medium, or high self-esteem? Explain.

No person is one-dimensional. There are three views of every individual—the view that God has of us, the opinions that others have of us, and the perception we have of ourselves. Though blemished by sin, we can regain our self-esteem through the process of spiritual regeneration.

What do these verses tell us about low self-esteem?

Isaiah 61:7

_____

2 Corinthians 3:1–5

_____

What have you learned about yourself from these verses?

_____

_____

_____

_____

_____

These Scriptures focus on God's positive view of us. If we believe them, then we should be able to move from negative (low) to positive (high) self-esteem.

Charles Stanley wrote, "Having a sense of security is more than simply building self-esteem. Jesus Christ is our genuine source of strength and confidence —if we attempt to overcome insecurity without Him, we will simply be masking it with our own efforts."[23]

Ezekiel, an aristocratic priest of Jerusalem, was among those carried captive to Babylon. His message to the people of Israel was that before they could ever hope to return to their beloved Jerusalem, they must first return to the Lord.

Read Ezekiel 16:4–19.

This passage paints an incredible picture of what God did for these people and how He feels about us.

Does any specific verse speak to you? Which ones? Why?

_____

_____

_____

_____

What does God tell you in verse 8 that demonstrates His love and ongoing commitment to you?

_____

_____

_____

_____

God talks about perfect beauty in verses 10–13. How do His words apply to your situation today?

_____

_____

_____

We have the power to choose to change our thinking if we want to. Do you want to stick your finger down your throat or wear a crown? Explain.

_____

_____

_____

Healing of low self-esteem will be not easy or immediate. We can dwell on our negative qualities and continue to put ourselves down, or we can receive with gratefulness God's design and love. God says, *I have the best for you.* God is saying, *You are mine. You are the daughter of the King!* Every little girl wants to be a princess . . . you have been a princess all along! When we realize we are princesses, we value ourselves differently—live differently. I became victorious over bulimia and my destructive behavior when I realized I was the daughter of the King.

Week Five: Your Mind is the Battlefield

Your spiritual life is under attack everyday.

Kristin said, "I have been in and out of therapy and treatment programs for too many years to count. I've read every self-help book. I have prayed relentlessly to God. Nothing ever changes. For eighteen years, my body has suffered. My pastor told me I was living in the enemy's camp. This enemy has turned me against myself by clouding my mind and filling me with pain, rage, and anger. He has sent people into my life who abuse, torment, and hurt me. The enemy has done everything in his power to keep me from God. And he is winning."

Kristin is at war. Satan is very real and hates all that God loves, and that includes you because God loves you. We can all probably say that we have underestimated the spiritual battles that rage around us every day. I always knew Satan existed but thought he'd be spending his time on more worthwhile people, like Billy Graham (well-known evangelist who ranked number seven on Gallup's list of admired people for the 20th century[24]). As long as we maintain our status quo, Satan will leave us in peace. But when we seek Christ with all our heart and start making changes to our lives, he will go on the attack, and we need the weapons to fight back!

Day One: Spiritual Warfare

~

Be aware! Satan will want to cloud your mind as you study the truth!

Satan's goal is to take our minds and hearts off Jesus Christ, then steer us to the "world's way." Jesus was tempted numerous times by Satan. Luke 4:1–12:

[1] Jesus, full of the Holy Spirit, returned from the Jordan and was led by the Spirit in the desert, [2] where for forty days he was tempted by the devil. He ate nothing during those days, and at the end of them he was hungry. [3] The devil said to him, "If you are the Son of God, tell this stone to become bread." [4] Jesus answered, "It is written: 'Man does not live on bread alone.'" [5] The devil led him up to a high place and showed him in an instant all the kingdoms of the world. [6] And he said to him, "I will give you all their authority and splendor, for it has been given to me, and I can give it to anyone I want to. [7] So if you worship me, it will all be yours." [8] Jesus answered, "It is written: Worship the Lord your God and serve him only." [9] The devil led him to Jerusalem and had him stand on the highest point of the temple. "If you are the Son of God," he said, "throw yourself down from here [10] For it is written: "He will command his angels concerning you to guard you carefully; [11] they will lift you up in their hands, so that you will not strike your foot against a stone." [12] Jesus answered, "It says: 'Do not put the Lord your God to the test'."

Satan first tried to get Jesus to slip by appealing to His need to relieve His hunger. Similarly, we are most tempted to slip back into our old behaviors and addictions when we are hungry, angry, lonely, tired, or depressed.

With each temptation that Satan offered, Jesus resisted by using the Word of God: "It is written . . ." As Satan tempts us, we need to fight with God's Word: "It is written . . ." Notice that Jesus' response was "low key." There was no wielding of swords or summoning angelic beings to fight. He used the simple, direct proclamation of the living Word of God. Can you see that the power is in God's Word, not in raising our voices or dramatic stances?

Luke 4:13 says, "When the devil had finished all this tempting, he left him until an opportune time." Satan will leave you when you resist him, but he always comes back. He waits for just the right moment. Satan was persistent in his attempts to get Jesus off track, and we will not find immunity either.

Since the dawn of man, we have messed up. Satan and his demon angels witnessed our sinful nature. There was no hope . . . until that morning when Jesus rose from the grave. Without the resurrection of Jesus Christ, there is nothing to celebrate. But Jesus did rise again, and He is the way.

Remember, God alone holds your destiny (destiny is not an end, but living out your purpose in life today). Satan's time is limited, and his destiny is assured. John said, "The prince of this world, shall be cast out" (John 12:31). Our attitude must be, "I can't defeat the devil, but I can resist him and *trust Jesus* to defeat him for me." God wants us to be wise, to be aware, to be informed, and to be ready. James 4:7 tells us how to resist: "Submit yourselves, then, to God. Resist the devil, and he will flee from you."

Jesus resisted Satan with the power of the Word of God. It was imprinted on His heart. That is why it is so important to commit to God's Word to our mind and heart so that we don't have to fight in our own strength. You are a child of God. The enemy has no business whispering lies into your mind—remind him of that!

> "Beware of no man more than yourself; we carry our worst enemies with us."
>
> –Charles Haddon Spurgeon (1834–1893)

Reflective Questions

How will you begin to recognize the difference between the truth and deception?

Think about how you can raise your awareness of the enemy. What can you do today to embrace consciously God's promises?

Day Two: Depression and Shame

~

Depression is a household word today.

Depression is called the "common cold of counseling." Twice as many women as men suffer from depression. Why? Satan has very cunningly led each person through a series of lies that they believed, and life eventually becomes mental torment.

Laura writes, "I feel myself slipping into a self-absorbed, secluded world. I'm shutting people out. I could break down in floods of tears at any moment. I feel so fragile and insignificant and a nuisance. I'm angry with everybody. I just want to be by myself. My head is such a mess. I'm confused and incredibly depressed."

To be depressed is to be "pressed down." There are various reasons we direct our emotions down—or inward—abuse, loss of a loved one, stress, pursuit of thinness, guilt, intense teasing, and/or rejection. Depression can also be a symptom of unbelief. We should to turn to God and ask Him to direct us.

> "God knows exactly where to meet you."
> –Edie, my friend and group leader

The Bible is full of people with broken hearts and spirits. King Ahab became depressed when he couldn't get his own way. When Ahab's neighbor refused to sell him a piece of property, he threw a temper tantrum and became "sullen and angry." He lay on his bed "sulking and refused to eat" (1 Kings 21:4).

Hannah, a godly woman, became depressed when she had to deal with a combination of unfulfilled longing and a strained relationship over a prolonged period of time. She had a godly husband, Elkanah, who loved her dearly. However, for reasons known only to the Lord, He had closed her womb. Hannah's struggles with barrenness were exacerbated by her husband's other wife, Peninnah (Elkanah had two wives). Peninnah had no difficulty conceiving and bearing children, and she "kept provoking Hannah in order to irritate her" (1 Samuel 1:6). For years, she provoked her until she wept and couldn't eat. Hannah was depressed (7).

One of my favorite promises for trouncing depression is John 8:12: "Jesus said, 'I am the light of the world. Whoever follows me will never walk in darkness, but will have the light of life.'" Did you get that? Jesus promises that if we accept Him and follow Him, we will never walk in darkness again. That's another truth!

Shame

Dr. Larry Crabb wrote,

The real killer of the self and the real cause of all addictions is shame. Shame is the experience of feeling deficient. Shame causes us to see our identity as flawed rather than seeing ourselves as having flaws. Our harsh judgments lead us to see ourselves as ugly, stupid, and fat. The result is a deep hole in the soul.[25]

Most of us have become ashamed of our behavior. I used to think that no normal person would put herself through this sort of monstrous ritual. I didn't tell anyone because of the potential rejection and embarrassment. As a binger, I did things only bag ladies did—steal food, eat discarded food, and mess up public toilets.

In an effort to protect ourselves, we try to hide our behavior because we are afraid of the answer to "the question," *Will you still love me now that you know?*

God gives us hope in His Word—promises that relieve shame.

• Psalms 25:2–3: "In you I trust, O my God. Do not let me be put to shame, nor let my enemies triumph over me. No one whose hope is in you will ever be put to shame, but they will be put to shame who are treacherous without excuse."

• Psalms 34:4–5: "I sought the Lord, and he answered me; he delivered me from all my fears. Those who look to him are radiant; their faces are never covered with shame."

Reflective Questions

What will you do differently this week to trounce the darkness and open the way to light?

Which emotions and situations are you ready to take to the cross and let Jesus carry for you so that you can be set free? Write a prayer to Jesus and tell Him exactly how you feel.

Day Three: Guilt and Isolation

~

Let me count the ways that I feel guilty!

I felt a tremendous amount of guilt when I skipped classes in college (an education my parents worked hard to pay for) to binge. I was a no-show for two weddings because I was hungover. Is it any wonder I had few friends? I felt tremendous guilt over giving sixteen years of my life to this monster.

In Psalm 38:4–11, David describes his feelings of guilt. Check the ones that you have personally experienced.

• Verse 4: "My guilt has overwhelmed me like a burden too heavy to bear."

• Verse 5: "My wounds fester and are loathsome because of my sinful folly."

• Verse 6: "I am bowed down and brought very low; all day long I go about mourning."

• Verse 7: "My back is filled with searing pain; there is no health in my body."

• Verse 8: "I am feeble and utterly crushed; I groan in anguish of heart."

• Verse 9: "All my longings lie open before you, O Lord; my sighing is not hidden from you."

• Verse 10: "My heart pounds, my strength fails me; even the light has gone from my eyes."

• Verse 11: "My friends and companions avoid me because of my wounds; my neighbors stay far away."

The Lord wants us to give Him all our guilt and shame. Many of us feel guilty for wasting valuable years focusing on ourselves and on our food addiction when we could have been participating in life-nurturing experiences. We can relieve and wash away our guilt. Psalms 32:5 tells us how: "Then *I acknowledged my sin to you* and did not cover up my iniquity. I said, "I will confess my transgressions *(sin or wrongdoings)* to the Lord"—and you forgave the guilt of my sin."

Isolation

Depression often leads to isolation or vice versa. Think of what it would be like to be one of those prisoners sentenced to solitary confinement. It's dark, cold, as close to living in a coffin as you can come. There's no way out. The loneliness. No solution.

Today, you may feel like you're in solitary confinement, and that's not a good feeling, is it? That's because God did not design us to be isolated. We were created in His image, made to have a relationship with Him and other people. However, many of us have become that prisoner in solitary confinement. And when we isolate ourselves from God and others, it is impossible to feel joy.

Psalm 107:10–11 tells us what the prisoners of that time felt and why: "Some sat in darkness and the deepest gloom, prisoners suffering in iron chains, for they had rebelled against the words of God and despised the counsel of the Most high."

I don't know anyone with an addiction that is not isolated. I would decline social invitations in lieu of a binge, and after awhile, people just stopped inviting me out. I stole hundreds of hours from my employer when I left my sales territory early to go home and binge—alone.

Psalms 107:13–14 tells us how the prisoners got out of their gloom: "Then they cried to the Lord in their trouble, and he saved them from their distress. He brought them out of darkness and the deepest gloom and broke away their chains."

We get more advice from Hebrews 3:13: "Encourage one another daily, as long as it is called Today, so that none of you may be hardened by sin's deceitfulness."

Encouraging one another helps to break down the walls. One day, my boyfriend told me I needed to make more friends because I was totally dependant on him (smothering). He was right. I began reconnecting with the world, slowly but surely.

God knows about our emotional isolation, and He answers our prayers by offering opportunities for connection with others. Don't miss that divine appointment He has set up for you! God can break those chains of bondage if you seek His counsel. That's why it's important to *take the time* to develop a personal relationship with God.

Reflective Questions

In what ways do you feel like those prisoners described in Psalm 107? How can you get out of your gloom?

Is there someone you want to encourage today? Take a moment or make a plan to do that.

Day Four: Satan's Games

~

We've tried to hide from God.

Max Lucado wrote,

When we kept our sin silent, we withdrew from Him (God). We saw Him as an enemy. We took steps to avoid His presence. But our confession of faults alters our perception. God is no longer a foe, but a friend. We are at peace with Him. Jesus was crushed for the evil we did. The punishment, which made us well, was given to Him. He accepted the shame. He leads us into the presence of God.[26]

The guilt, shame, and isolation is too much to bear. The only way for us to find freedom is to come to our Lord, confess our sins, and seek a new life through Him. Think of confession as part of maintaining a healthy relationship with God.

As we turn our life over to God, Satan will more than likely bring lying thoughts into our minds to make us fearful of surrendering. He'll say that if we give control to God, then we'll be condemned from joy in our life. That's simply not true! God is not in the business of condemning His children—that's Satan's business. God's business is to liberate us and draw us closer to Him. My life is complete, fun, and full of joy now that I have given myself to the Lord. Satan did stymie me for a long time because I wasn't wise to his tactics. Part of our new life requires becoming prudent to Satan's games and tactics.

"What If . . ." "If Only . . ."

Even after I healed from bulimia, Satan never stopped playing with my mind—the "what if/what might have been" game. My mind became Satan's hunting ground as I thought about how my life would have been different if I hadn't wasted all those years as a bulimic and party-girl. Like so many other women, I wanted the "American Dream." Married at twenty-something to a successful doctor or lawyer. Living a sweet life like I saw on "Leave It To Beaver" and "The Cosby Show." Satan preyed on this. He made me believe that I had disappointed God and was not a pure woman.

That's his tactic—to get us to not only doubt ourselves but also doubt, ignore, and disobey God's Word and His love. "What if?" Just two words. I constantly said, "*What if* they don't like me?" "*What if* I lose my job?" "*What if* I fail?" "*What if* I'm left alone?" "*What if* I'm not good enough?" "*What if* they think I'm ugly?" "*What if* no one ever falls in love with me?" Two small words, yet loaded with dread, fear, and anxiety.

Two more powerful words: "If only." Two words that say, "If my circumstances were different, I would be different." My life was full of "if onlys." "*If only* I was prettier." "*If only* I was thinner." "*If only* I was married." "*If only* I was smarter." The list went on . . .

A fact of life is that not everyone is going to love or accept us the way we are. As hard as we try, we can't be perfect, so we have to deal with rejection. How do we handle that?

The apostle Paul said, "We take captive every thought to make it obedient to Christ" (2 Corinthians 10:5). When God says, "Take *every* thought captive," He doesn't mean dissect every single thought. He means *stop!* Take a good, hard look at the *big, nasty* ones: the anxious ones, hurtful ones, doubtful ones, the frustrations, anger, pride, gossip, and jealousy. Take them to Him. We also tell the enemy we are not going to debate this with him anymore. Remember, we are continuously being conformed into Jesus' image.

> "Deliverance finally comes when you confront your past and put it in its proper perspective. It happened to you but it is not you. You survived the trauma; you too can walk again."
>
> –Serita Ann Jakes[27]

Rejection

Everyday I try to learn from my mistakes and seek to turn from that which is not Christ-like. When I feel rejection, I remember that Jesus, who was perfect, was rejected. Even Jesus' own brothers did not believe in Him (John 7:5). I am God's servant, not man's. Hebrews 13:5–6 (a good memory verse) says: "Keep your lives free from the love of money and be content with what you have, because God has said, 'Never will I leave you; never will I forsake you.'" [6] So we say with confidence, "The Lord is my helper; I will not be afraid. What can man do to me?"

God will *never* leave us, nor forsake us. We are accepted no matter what. Man will reject us. There may be times we think the Lord has forgotten about us. Times when the pain, hurt, and rejection are really bad. What do we do? Run to the Word, and remember that God loves you with an everlasting love. God *will not, and cannot,* reject His own children.

2 Timothy 1:7 says that God did not give us a spirit of timidity (*fear*), but a spirit of power, of love, and of self-discipline (*sound mind*). That means that any fear, any shaken confidence like rejection, comes from Satan. Does he have power over you? No. Satan has *no* power over Christians; we have the authority to tell him to leave us alone. "It is written . . ."

Confession

We keep hearing the term "confess your sins." Confess means

to talk about—bring out into the open. Proverbs 28:13 says, "He who conceals his sins does not prosper, but whoever confesses and renounces them finds mercy."

☑ If you haven't done so, take the time to confess your sins to God and ask for forgiveness. The Lord has promised to forgive you immediately—as if you've never sinned before. Personally, I took quite a bit of time and wrote all the sins I could think of on a piece of paper, prayed over them, and then burned the list.

Day Five: Dressing for Battle

The battle begins!

Now that we know who the enemy is, we have to fight him! Every soldier knows the time to put on armor is *before* being attacked—not after the fight begins.

God did something that was right up my alley. He told me how to dress. No, we didn't go shopping (darn), but through Scripture, He told me what to wear:

> [11] *Put on the full armor of God so that you can take your stand against the devil's schemes.* [12] *For our struggle is not against flesh and blood, but against the rulers, against the authorities, against the powers of this dark world and against the spiritual forces of evil in the heavenly realms.* [13] *Therefore put on the full armor of God, so that when the day of evil comes, you may be able to stand your ground, and after you have done everything, to stand (Ephesians 6:11–13).*

This passage clearly states *we are at war*. We are also told how to dress *everyday* for battle (sorry, pink stilettos aren't part of the dress code).

The Dress Code for Battle

> [14] *Stand firm then, with the belt of truth buckled around your waist, with the breastplate of righteousness in place,* [15] *and with your feet fitted with the readiness that comes from the gospel of peace.* [16] *In addition to all this, take up the shield of faith, with which you can extinguish all the flaming*

arrows of the evil one. [17] *Take the helmet of salvation and the sword of the Spirit, which is the word of God (Ephesians 6:14–18).*

The Belt of Truth

The belt of truth is one of our primary weapons of defense because our adversary is the father of all lies. We can probably say we've become good liars, and our culture seems to accept that. But a lie is a lie. Truth is our first line of defense against the enemy. If we lie, no matter how small, we are abandoning the belt of truth.

It is *so important* that we hold fast to the truth. Truth must be the filter for all perceptions, ideas, and even dreams. We are now starting to learn how to sift through the culture's messages that bombard us every day. We throw them out if the message doesn't line up with God's truth.

Breastplate of Righteousness

The breastplate offered great protection and covered the heart, just like the righteousness of Christ covers us and protects us. Isaiah 59:17 says, "He put on righteousness as his breastplate." We do the same. By ourselves, we have no righteousness; we are only clothed in righteousness when we are in Christ.

The breastplate guards our emotions and protects our heart. We bring into our life things that are pure—nothing polluting. When Satan whispers to you that you are not worthy of God's love, that you can never get better, that you are a loser, come into God's presence in the name of Jesus.

Boots of Peace

In the beginning, a wicked angel named Lucifer (the serpent) came to Eve. His objective was to drive a wedge between God and His children. Hundreds of years later, the angel Gabriel came from

God, delivering good news to Mary of Nazareth that through her son, Jesus, our relationship with God would be restored. Today, we have our own boots of peace with God through Jesus, and that gives us victory in this war.

Shield of Faith

Our faith in God is our protection against those fiery darts (ugly thoughts and lies) that Satan throws at us. When he lies to us, tempts us, and accuses us, we hold up the shield the faith. We deflect his fiery darts and extinguish them for good. 1 Peter 5:8–9: "Your enemy the devil prowls around like a roaring lion looking for someone to devour. Resist him, standing firm in the faith."

Faith is a two-sided weapon. When we step out to do something, it is our *faith* and our *belief* that God has called us to do it. We believe He will equip us to do it. Without the shield of faith, the rest of the armor will *not* work.

The Sword of the Spirit

The sword of the Spirit is the only weapon of offense that we have. It is the Word of God—living and powerful. If we don't know God's Word, then we don't know His ways and how to get help from Him. When Satan lies, we speak the truth. Speaking the truth stops him from running rampant in our lives. When we walk in truth, we make decisions according to God's plans, not Satan's.

The Sword of the Spirit is our manual of faith, the hope we're all looking for. God's Word also functions in a powerful way as a mirror. Scripture enables us to see ourselves as we really are—it exposes wrong behaviors and our heart condition.

Helmet of Salvation

The helmet of salvation protects our minds. Paul wrote in 1 Thessalonians 5:6–8,

So then, let us not be like others, who are asleep, but let us be alert and self-controlled. For those who sleep, sleep at night, and those who get drunk, get drunk at night. But since we belong to the day, let us be self-controlled, putting on faith and love as a breastplate, and the hope of salvation as a helmet.

Paul reminds us that our salvation is secure in Christ. Satan will say we don't deserve salvation because he wants to separate us from God. We put on our helmet of salvation, which is God's promise to us. We belong to Him, and *nothing* can separate us from His love.

The armor works. The enemy will strike! It's not a matter of "if"—it's "when." We should each put our armor on before our feet hit the floor in the morning. When we put the full armor of God on, we put on the nature of Christ, which means we are *dressed to kill!* You say to Satan, "You have to go through Jesus to get to me!"

Over time, the battle will get easier. The reason we fail is because we wait until the hour of the battle. Those that succeed gain victory in prayer long before the battle begins. My advice is to pray the "Warrior's Prayer" every morning:

Lord, Help me to remember as I face life's challenges that an unseen battle is going on for my spiritual life. Send your Holy Spirit to give me the wisdom to recognize what is the truth and what is a lie. Remind me that the best way to win the battles of my mind is in prayer and by reading Your Word.

To prepare myself for the battle ahead, by faith I put on Your armor:

I am thankful for the Armor You have provided. I put on the Belt of Truth, the Breastplate of Righteousness, the Boots of Peace, and the Helmet of Salvation. I lift up the Shield of Faith against all the fiery darts of the enemy; and I take in my hand the Sword of the Spirit, the Word of God. I put on this Armor and live and pray in complete dependence upon You.

Thank you for assuring me of victory today. I surrender all to You today and let You fight for me. If You are with me, I know nothing can hurt me, and I can be transformed. So by faith, I claim victory over my life! In Jesus' name I pray, Amen.

Reflective Questions

Twice God tells us to put on "the whole armor of God" (11, 13). Why do we so easily ignore these instructions (instead, we show up in those pink stilettos)?

How will the armor of God be effective in your healing process?

Finale: Week Five

~

Nothing less than the "God of all comfort" can meet our deepest needs.

"The Lord is my rock, my fortress and my deliverer; my God is my rock, in whom I take refuge. He is my shield and the horn of my salvation, my stronghold. I call to the Lord, who is worthy of praise, and I am saved from my enemies" (Psalm 18:2–3).

We need to *submit completely* to God because we are not merely fighting against food, behavior patterns, substances, or dysfunctional people—we are fighting an enemy. When Satan is knocking at your door, simply say, "Jesus, could You get that for me?" Philippians 4:19 reminds us: "My God will meet all your needs."

What did you learn from this week's study that you can apply to your life this week?

> Promise to Claim: "Put on the full armor of God so that you can take your stand against the devil's schemes"
> (Ephesians 6:11).

I Want More Bible Food!
Week Five: Your Mind is the Battlefield

~

2 Corinthians 10:3–7

Describe a time you felt you were in a battle. What weapons did you use to fight, and how effective were they?

☑ Some of the most powerful weapons in Satan's arsenal are psychological: fear, doubt, anger, hostility, worry, and guilt. An uneasy sense of self-condemnation hangs over many of us like a dark cloud. We find ourselves defeated by the most powerful psychological weapon that Satan uses. Low self-esteem is one great example.

2 Corinthians 10:3–7: *I recommend memorizing this passage.*

³ For though we live in the world, we do not wage war as the world does. ⁴ The weapons we fight with are not the weapons of the world. On the contrary, they have divine power to demolish strongholds. ⁵ We demolish arguments and every pretension that sets itself up against the knowledge of God, and we take captive every thought to make it obedient to Christ. ⁶ And we will be ready to punish every act of disobedience, once your obedience is complete. ⁷ You are looking only on the surface of things. If anyone is confident that he belongs to Christ, he should consider again that we belong to Christ just as much as he.

Mark every use of the pronoun *we,* and then record what you have learned about.

I'm Beautiful, Why Can't I See It? | 131

What does verse 4 tell you?

_____

_____

_____

_____

In verse 7, what were the Corinthians doing that they shouldn't have been doing?

_____

_____

_____

_____

The Cycle of Depression

When we get depressed, our eyes turn inward, and we focus on all our problems and ourselves. The more we focus on the inside, the worse we feel, and the harder it becomes to seek necessary help.

What advice do the following Scriptures give on how we can break this cycle?

Where should your eyes be focused? Hebrews 12:1–2

_____

_____

Where should your mind be focused? Colossians 3:2

_____

_____

What does Ephesians 4:22–24 tell us?

_____

_____

Which of these verses will you remember in times of depression?

_____

_____

How can you apply them to your life *today?*

_____

_____

_____

_____

_____

Week Six: The Heart of Anger

[Step Eight]

~

Anger. Resentment. Grudges. Bitterness.

We all have these emotions, but sometimes we are held captive to them when left unresolved. As women, we learn to silence our anger, to deny it entirely, or to vent it in a way that leaves us feeling helpless and powerless. We can suppress it, deny it, and allow it to control us or *learn to manage it.*

Anger is powerful. The dictionary says it is *a strong feeling of displeasure or hostility*[28]. When it arises, we respond. Anger is an inward emotion caused by an outward action, circumstance, or situation. This action, circumstance, or situation may be something we do or do not do. Or it may be something done apart from us or done to us. These emotions just don't go away. Denied, they express themselves in symptoms like depression and overeating.

Your issues with food and self-image may be a symptom of anger. You may not even recognize that you have stored up that much emotion. Sometime and somewhere in the past, you were deeply hurt by someone. Those of us with abnormal eating habits tend to turn that hurt inward.

Dr. Gregory Jantz said,

For some reason you couldn't direct that anger at the person responsible for your pain, so it stayed within you. Anger, improperly directed and unexpressed leads to resentment. Resentment has festered into self-destructive eating. Confronting your anger and those who caused it will free you for the next step, forgiveness.[29]

The good news is that anger channeled positively is a good thing. Think of it like a gas flame on your stovetop. That flame isn't destructive when it's is used properly. Used correctly, the flame is a good thing for cooking our food. Used improperly, that flame can be harmful and destructive. We can learn to express our anger in healthy ways.

Day One: God's Anger

~

God gets angry too.

Ellie is mad at her dad for bringing her up in bars and then turning his back when her uncle raped her. Today, seventeen years later, Ellie loses control in fits of rage and manages to destroy everything good in her life. Jana is angry because her father molested her, resulting in pregnancy. I would say these women's anger is justified. More importantly, it makes God angry too.

Over time, these women came to forgive their fathers. Consequently, God has done some miraculous things in their lives. Each woman has come to terms with her weight and body image. Ellie no longer binges and purges. Jana does not overeat anymore. God healed them, and He can heal you. For these women, it all began when they became willing to give their anger to God.

In the Bible, there are many examples of God expressing His anger:

• Deuteronomy 29:28: "In furious anger and in great wrath the Lord uprooted them from their land and thrust them into another land, as it is now."

• Psalms 78:49: "He unleashed against them his hot anger, his wrath, indignation, and hostility—a band of destroying angels."

• Psalms 90:7: "We are consumed by your anger and terrified by your indignation."

Yes, our God is the God of unconditional love, but there are things He hates. Proverbs 6:16–19 tells us there are six things the Lord hates; seven that are detestable to Him:

Haughty (proud, arrogant, over-conceited) eyes

A lying tongue

Hands that shed innocent blood

A heart that devises wicked schemes

Feet that are quick to rush into evil

A false witness who pours out lies

A man who stirs up dissension among brothers

Yet, God is slow to anger:

• Psalms 78:38: "Yet he was merciful; he forgave their iniquities and did not destroy them. Time after time, he restrained his anger and did not stir up his full wrath."

• Exodus 34:6–7: "The Lord, the compassionate and gracious God, slow to anger, abounding in love and faithfulness, maintaining love to thousands, and forgiving wickedness, rebellion and sin."

God's anger is mighty and very powerful. This is righteous anger. It is justified and only provoked by sin and disobedience. One cannot read the Old Testament without seeing God's anger. His wrath is as great as the fear that is due Him.

The good news is we are saved from God's wrath, and we experience His forgiveness through Calvary (Acts 13:38, Romans 5:8–11, 1 Thessalonians 2:10).

"Getting angry can sometimes be like leaping into a wonderfully responsive sports car, gunning the motor, taking off at high speed and then discovering the brakes are out of order."

—Maggie Scarf[30]

Reflective Questions

Do you think God is angry with you for similar acts that have been described in Proverbs 6:16–19? Reread the list carefully.

Should you be afraid of God's anger? Why or why not?

What did you learn about God's anger? What is the root of His anger?

Day Two: Jesus' Anger

Jesus Christ, in the flesh, felt anger.

He had the same emotions we do. He became angry when He saw others commit wrongdoings, but He used it to see that justice was served. There were two difficult times that Jesus was righteously angry. Yet, He was righteously controlled. We know from the Bible that Jesus always handled His anger in a way pleasing to God, because He only said and did things that pleased God.

What was the cause of Jesus' anger in John 2:13–16?

[13] *When it was almost time for the Jewish Passover, Jesus went up to Jerusalem.* [14] *In the temple courts he found men selling cattle, sheep and doves, and others sitting at tables exchanging money.* [15] *So he made a whip out of cords, and drove all from the temple area, both sheep and cattle; he scattered the coins of the money changers and overturned their tables.* [16] *To those who sold doves he said, "Get these out of here! How dare you turn my Father's house into a market!"*

Notice that Jesus carefully planned and executed His response. He was in complete control. Verse 15 says He made a whip out of cords. That is a time-consuming project—time Jesus most likely used to think and control His anger. If you were there, how would you have responded?

What made Jesus angry in Mark 3:1–6, and how did He express His feelings?

[1] *Another time he went into the synagogue, and a man with a shriveled*

hand was there. ² *Some of them were looking for a reason to accuse Jesus, so they watched him closely to see if he would heal him on the Sabbath.* ³ *Jesus said to the man with the shriveled hand, "Stand up in front of everyone."* ⁴ *Then Jesus asked them, "Which is lawful on the Sabbath: to do good or to do evil, to save life or to kill?" But they remained silent.* ⁵ *He looked around at them in anger and, deeply distressed at their stubborn hearts, said to the man, "Stretch out your hand." He stretched it out, and his hand was completely restored.* ⁶ *Then the Pharisees went out and began to plot with the Herodians how they might kill Jesus.*

Again, Jesus was totally in control. He continued with the healing instead of verbally showing His distress. Jesus did express His emotions. His expression of anger was always righteous because He was righteous. Can you say the same about yourself?

Our anger isn't always righteous because we are not always righteous. Our emotions can be destructive, destroying people, and relationships. However, we can learn to model Jesus. Jesus made use of His anger. He used it against wrong. When He saw people being victimized by evil of any kind, or saw God's will being thwarted, Jesus got angry. So it follows that anger serves a useful purpose when it leads to positive action.

We must follow Jesus' example. What have we learned? Justified or not, anger is never to control us. *We are to be controlled by the Spirit of God.* Therefore, our response to anger must be according to Jesus' character. *A person with good sense is patient, and it is to his credit that he overlooks an offense* (Proverbs 19:11).

Reflective Questions

What rejection, hurt, or disappointment might be driving your anger? What about your abnormal eating patterns that makes you angry?

How do you think Jesus wants you to express your emotions? Will you rest in Jesus and put a halt to the anger?

Day Three: Our Anger

~

Anger hurts because it makes us suffer.

When something or someone makes us mad and we deny or ignore it, we become angry or resentful. The key to preventing and letting go is to start expressing our feelings either verbally or in writing. This is not an attempt to change the other person but to unload the poison of resentment from ourselves.

Why Do We Get Angry?

When others do not deal fairly with us. In 1 Samuel 25:1–34, David protected Nabal's flocks, but Nabal would not return the favor by giving David's men a share of his harvest. That made David angry, and in return, he set out to destroy Nabal. It was Abigail (Nabal's wife), who brought David to his senses when she asked him to forgive Nabal (28). And David did forgive Nabal and brought his anger under God's control. And God ultimately dealt with Nabal.

When we see others being mistreated. In 1 Samuel 20, Jonathan's feelings toward his father, King Saul, portrays anger when we see others not treated properly. Jonathon was angry over Saul's treatment of David. Perhaps you can relate to Jonathan if you have a family member that is abusive or you live with an angry person. The anger that you have must be dealt with, for the Bible says to *harbor anger is sin*. It's a fact that this pent up anger can cause you to mistreat others, perhaps your own children.

Because of the sin of others. In Exodus, Moses experienced this type of anger many times while he led the children of Israel.

Jealousy. In 1 Samuel 18:7–8, Saul's response to the praise given David was, "They have credited David with tens of thousands but me with only thousands." This is jealous anger. Saul wanted to kill David because of this. There's that mask of jealousy, and we get angry when that *someone else* is successful and happy because we are not successful or happy. Can you see how critical it is that we deal with our anger?

Pressure, interruption, irritation, or inconvenience in our lives. 1 Samuel 17:28–29 is another example of anger when David visits his brothers while Goliath is challenging their army.

When we cannot fulfill someone else's expectations. Genesis 30:2 portrays Rachel getting upset with Jacob because he does not give her children. Can't we all point to a parent, friend, or mate that hurt us because they could not fulfill our expectations? Then what happened? We became angry with that person.

Having our sins exposed by others. When we sin, we don't want to be found out, do we? If we are found out, watch out! The fury can be great. We see this in Numbers 22:21–35 when Balaam beats his donkey.

Personal pride. Pride is of the flesh, so when our pride is hurt, we may become angry. In 2 Chronicles 25:10, when King Amaziah sent home a group of soldiers before they were ever allowed to fight in a battle, the soldiers became angry.

When someone embarrasses us. Many times people will turn against their mate or best friend and seek to hurt them because they have been humiliated and/or embarrassed. In the book of Esther, King Ahasuerus was angry when Vashti would not do as he asked. She embarrassed him (Esther 2).

Condemnation causes anger. In Job 32:1–5, Elihu's anger against Job and his three friends for justifying himself rather than God illustrates this type of anger.

> "Do not lose courage in considering your own imperfections, but instantly set about remedying them—every day begin the task anew."
>
> –St. Francis de Sales (1567–1622)

Reflective Questions

Can you think of someone right now who fits any of these scenarios? Often, we say things, or someone else says something, that will haunt us for a long time. Worst yet, the anger becomes physical. Don't turn to anger or frustration because the damage can be irreparable. *Instead, turn to God and talk to Him about your anger.* Write a prayer now.

Negative feelings cause a crushed spirit (and open us up to the schemes of Satan). How can you know if your negative feelings or anger have not been dealt with and released to God? What will you change from this day on? For example, how will you address these feelings versus pushing them down?

Day Four: . . At Our Parents

I hate my parents!

Quite often, the people that are responsible for our anger are the people we love most, our parents. Often, they are not even aware of their actions.

Angie said, "My dad says that I'm just sinning, and all I need to do is repent in order to eat normal again. My sinning makes him mad, and he makes me mad."

I have something for you to think about if this is you. Perhaps you experienced some form of physical, sexual, emotional, and/or spiritual neglect or abuses. Without the neglect or abuse committed against you, it is possible to conclude that your issues with food and self may not have developed.

Most often, we turn to food and substances as a way to meet a rational human need—love and acceptance. Please don't let anyone blame you for trying to meet your basic human needs.

Our Parents Example

As we grew up, the way our parents handled their anger was an example to us. We can come to understand how their example has influenced our emotions.

> "God does not love us because we are valuable, but we are valuable because God loves us."
>
> —Martin Luther[31]

On the other hand, maybe there is no one you are angry with except yourself. You should be! Look at what this monster has done. It's robbed you of life! Heather says, "I'm so angry with myself for wasting my life like this. I am angry at my mind for feeding me self-loathing thoughts. But most of all, I am angry at myself for lacking the strength to beat this." Heather has the right to feel mad and sad. Emotional eating is a *loss* of life.

Reflective Questions

1. How did your father express his anger? Give some examples of what he usually said or what he did (actions). What about your mother?

2. What was it like for you to be around each of your parents when they were mad?

3. How do you express anger?

4. When you are angry, can you see your parents' traits coming out of you?

5. Which parent are you most like?

6. Ask those who are intimate with you to help you answer this question: What is it like for others to be around you when you are mad?

7. How would you like to express anger differently?

Day Five: . . . At God

I am so angry with God right now!

Terry continues, "I feel like He is punishing me all the time and wants me to suffer. I am angry that I am not worth a miracle. I have suffered long enough and have sincerely tried to change. I feel like I will never get well. Why won't God help me?"

How do you treat God when you're angry? One cannot be angry with God and be healed. That anger is never justifiable.

Why Would Anyone Get Angry With God?

We get angry with God when we see or feel suffering. Job is a person with whom we all can identify with in some way. His sufferings equate to Christ on the cross. I think we have all had a taste of the cross, of being crushed. The theme in the book of Job is one of suffering, but the *real story* is primarily about faith and *the role that suffering plays on faith.* The actual plan that falls apart is not God's; it's Satan's. *God does not plan for bad things to happen to us.*

We get angry with God when He doesn't conform to our ways or understanding. Cain got angry with God. In Genesis 4:1–8, Cain wanted to worship God his way, and he became angry when God rejected his sacrificial offering. If other people or circumstances have hurt you, you may be angry with God because you don't understand why a God of love would allow such things to happen to you or someone you love dearly. We all know of someone who has lost a child, and we are not surprised that they would be angry with God for the loss of their child.

We get angry with God because of His judgment. David got mad at God. In 1 Chronicles 13:9–11, David gets angry because God kills Uzi for touching the Ark of the Covenant. In the book of Revelation, men get mad at God for His judgments upon the earth. Today, there are many people who are suffering because of the consequences of their own sin. Yet, they have become angry with God because He judged them after they broke His commandments.

We become angry with God because we want Him to judge others fairly. In Jonah 1:1–11, Jonah got mad at God because God wouldn't destroy the Ninevites, whom he hated. Think about all the people who were angry and bitter towards God for allowing the Holocaust. Why didn't God destroy Hitler before he committed all of those terrible atrocities? We won't know until we meet God in eternity.

> "Let no one ever come to you without leaving better and happier."
>
> -Mother Teresa[32]

How does one deal with anger toward God? God tells us in Isaiah 45:20–24:

[20] *"Gather together and come; assemble, you fugitives from the nations. Ignorant are those who carry about idols of wood, who pray to gods that cannot save.* [21] *Declare what is to be, present it—let them take counsel together. Who foretold this long ago, who declared it from the distant past? Was it not I, the Lord? And there is no God apart from me, a righteous God and a Savior; there is none but me.* [22] *"Turn to me and be saved, all you ends of the earth; for I am God, and there is no other.* [23] *By myself I have sworn, my mouth has uttered in all integrity a word that will not be revoked: Before me every knee will bow; by me every tongue will swear.* [24] *They will say of me, 'In the Lord alone are righteousness and strength.' All who have raged against him will come to him and be put to shame.*

☑ What do you think the results will be if you don't release your anger to God? Ask the Holy Spirit to search your heart to see if you have any unresolved anger against God or anyone else. If He doesn't show you anything, then pray for others doing this study. Write down anything that God brings to mind.

If You Are Angry With God

State your case. Be angry at God if you must. Tell him what you're angry about. Use colorful language if you want. God isn't hurt by your anger. If you wrote anything down, talk to God about it.

Turn to God. Tell Him what's on your mind. He is your Father. But also remember, as His child, He isn't responsible to answer to you. When you were a kid, how many times did you hear, "When you're the parent, you can make all the decisions," "I'm the parent," and, "I don't answer to you"?

Put to shame your pride (24). Again, bring any unconfessed sin to Him. Maybe you've said that God is wrong in what He's done; there's something wrong with His character. That's playing judge and jury. It's pride and needs to be dealt with.

Humble yourself. "For us there is only one Lord, one faith, one baptism, and we all have the same God and Father who is over us all and in us all, and living through every part of us" (Ephesians 4:5–6, TLB).

Reflective Questions

What issues are you trying to hide?

Has God been speaking to you about your anger?

☑ Anger Letter
Here God's Word tells us that anger cannot be hidden or denied—it must be addressed immediately. Bring your anger out of

the darkness and into the light. Ask God to show you any bitterness. Complete this letter to God in your journal. If you are angry with more than one person, write a separate letter to each person. If you are part of a group, be prepared to read one of the letters at your next meeting.

Dear God, I'm angry with _____
for _____ . _____ hurt   me
when _____ .

Finale: Week Six

~

Anger can be useful and valuable.

As long as we know what to do with our anger, peace, rather than bitterness, will come as we trust God and wait patiently. That's the hardest part, to wait patiently until He brings it to pass. One day, you'll see God face to face despite your anger. Look forward to that moment when everything, even your suffering, will be erased by His presence.

Don't allow man to frustrate you or cause you to do sinful things. Trust is the key. Trust in God, the One who causes all things to work together for good. Trust is the healing balm for anger.

☑ Have hidden issues of anger surfaced as you completed this week? Write: "One thing I learned about anger is(note to Layout: long line here)."

Promise to Claim: "In your anger do not sin: Do not let the sun go down while you are still angry, and do not give the devil a foothold" (Ephesians 4:26–27).

I Want More Bible Food!
Week Six: The Heart of Anger

~

John 19

What are some of the benefits of expressing anger rather than internalizing it?

☑ We all handle anger differently. It may be an attempt to get back at others in an effort to hurt them as they hurt us. We often think God wouldn't approve of their act—then we feel justified for our anger. Let's look at Jesus.

When Jesus was sentenced to be crucified, Pilate said, "Where do you come from?" Jesus gave him no answer. "Do you refuse to speak to me?" Pilate said. "Don't you realize I have power either to free you or to crucify you?" (John 19:9–10).

16 Finally Pilate handed him over to them to be crucified. So the soldiers took charge of Jesus. 17 Carrying his own cross, he went out to the place of the Skull (which in Aramaic is called Golgotha). 18 Here they crucified him, and with him two others—one on each side and Jesus in the middle (John 19:16–18).

What did Jesus do to avenge His enemies as they set to crucify Him? Nothing. He didn't put up a fight. He had the weapons. He could have squashed them like a bug, but He didn't.

What does the Bible tell us about getting even? Read:

Matthew 5:38–42

_____

_____

Proverbs 24:17–18

_____

_____

Romans 12:19

_____

_____

2 Thessalonians 1:6–7

_____

_____

What are some ways that God wants us to respond? Look up:

Romans 12:20–21 (Each time I read this verse, I think of Mellie in "Gone With The Wind")

_____

_____

Ephesians 4:32

_____

_____

Colossians 3:13–14

_____

_____

Don't try to get even. Rejoice that Jesus took your hurts to the cross! As citizens of God's kingdom, we are not to be vigilantes. Our obligation is to love.

Week Seven: Peace With God

Emotional eating is about control.

Tamara writes, "I am a control freak probably because so many things in my life are outside of my control. The one thing that I can control is my body, my weight, and what I put into it. I am addicted to food, and binging is my way of acting out, escaping uncomfortable feelings, and saying I hate my life. Purging is control too. It's like acting like God and evading responsibility. I can rebel, and the rules do not apply to me."

Because of a variety of family and sociocultural influences, we've turned to food to cope and gain some semblance of management over our lives. Food is where we can take total charge of what we put into, or don't put into, our bodies. However, this is a false sense of control.

Growing up, our family moved often, and with each new school I started, I met rejection. I was also told what to do and failed numerous times. In my mind, that meant I lost control. I took to controlling the only thing I could—my own body. As a bulimic, I could ingest thousands of calories and not gain a pound. That was a powerful feeling (a high), to eat whatever I wanted, when I wanted, without suffering the consequences of getting fat.

My friend, Julie (who was anorexic), took control by saying "no" to food. Cathy, a compulsive overeater, kept others away from her by isolating herself in her room with food. *Abnormal eating isn't really about food as much as it's about taking control of the act of eating and trying to manage the associated pain.*

We develop issues of control in order to protect ourselves from pain. If you were abused in any form, constantly rejected, or had a controlling parent, you probably felt unable to curtail what was happening to you, so you turned to food, drugs, alcohol, and/or sex to deaden the pain. You may think you are in complete control, but are you?

No. They are only temporary fixes (Satan's stronghold) that hide the truth—the truth about the source of the pain.

On the other hand, being out of control can be a good thing! And that's when we are experiencing God's control in and over our lives.

Day One: Who is in Control?

Help has to come from a power greater than us.

When we deny our powerlessness over food, our lives become unmanageable. Amy writes, "My life has become unmanageable because I need to control my food intake in a vain attempt to control how I look and as a way to feel accepted and good enough. I have no control over food whatsoever because my food obsession has taken over my life, and therefore, it controls me. I know it's deception."

Satan has convinced us that we are in control of our own lives. The Bible tells us we should be careful who we listen to and choose our role models to be, "For Satan himself masquerades as an angel of light" (2 Corinthians 11:14). By accepting our powerlessness and unmanageability, we are accepting that we cannot take back our life alone. Who should we give control to and why? Yes, God. Romans 8:31: "If God is for us, who can be against us."

The real breakthrough for Amy was when she finally saw how the issue of control had been dominating her life. She realized that she wanted power over every situation and person in her life. It wasn't easy. When she released full control to God, a huge burden was lifted off her shoulders, and she began to change slowly. Amy began gaining weight because she trusted God to help her eat healthy. Over time, balance and stability were restored to her life.

Control is also a direct response to our fear, anger, family, and sense of helplessness. It happens when we feel overwhelmed or lose trust. We usually don't trust life, God, or ourselves. Instead of trusting, we revert to control. We can approach this by learning to have faith in ourselves, in God, and in a support group. This is healing.

One of the most difficult things about giving our all to God is relinquishing control. Many ask, "Can the person being controlled by food really be healed?" Dr. Gregory Jantz says, "Yes! There is something amazing that occurs when past hurts are resolved, and the substitute of food is no longer needed . . . They take back the control over their lives that they've given over to food."[33]

The parable of the sower teaches us about the development of abnormal eating patterns:

[5] *A farmer went out to sow his seed. As he was scattering the seed, some fell along the path; it was trampled on, and the birds of the air ate it up.* [6] *Some fell on rock, and when it came up, the plants withered because they had no moisture.* [7] *Other seed fell among thorns, which grew up with it and choked the plants.* [8] *Still other seed fell on good soil. It came up and yielded a crop, a hundred times more than was sown. When he said this, he called out, "He who has ears to hear, let him hear."* [9] *His disciples asked him what this parable meant.* [10] *He said, "The knowledge of the secrets of the kingdom of God has been given to you, but to others I speak in parables, so that, though seeing, they may not see; though hearing, they may not understand."* [11] *This is the meaning of the parable: The seed is the word of God.* [12] *Those along the path are the ones who hear, and then the devil comes and takes away the word from their hearts, so that they may not believe and be saved.* [13] *Those on the rock are the ones who receive the word with joy when they hear it, but they have no root. They believe for a while, but in the time of testing they fall away.* [14] *The seed that fell among thorns stands for those who hear, but as they go on their way they are choked by life's worries, riches and pleasures, and they do not mature.* [15] *But the seed on good soil stands for those with a noble and good heart, who hear the word, retain it, and by persevering produce a crop.*

☑ Where are you? On the path? The rock? Among the thorns? Or on the good soil? Explain in your journal.

We don't know what God has in store for us. We're fearful it may be too difficult or uncomfortable, or we won't be able to measure up. There is something to be said, literally, about letting God manage our lives:

• Proverbs 3:5–8:

[5] *Trust in the Lord with all your heart and lean not on your own understanding;* [6] *in all your ways acknowledge him, and he will make your paths straight.* [7] *Do not be wise in your own eyes; fear the Lord and shun evil.* [8] *This will bring health to your body and nourishment to your bones."*

• Psalms 18:16–20:

[16] *He reached down from on high and took hold of me; he drew me out of deep waters.* [17] *He rescued me from my powerful enemy, from my foes, who were too strong for me.* [18] *They confronted me in the day of my disaster, but the Lord was my support.* [19] *He brought me out into a spacious place; he rescued me because he delighted in me.* [20] *The Lord has dealt with me according to my righteousness; according to the cleanness of my hands he has rewarded me.*

> What beautiful promises! This may seem overwhelming, but God will give you the strength to do this.
>
> "Great things are not done by impulse, but by a series of small things brought together."
>
> –Vincent van Gogh (1853–1890)

Reflective Questions

What are you trying to take control of when you binge, or purge, or restrict yourself from eating? Finish this sentence: *When I feel I'm losing control, I control my outward self by doing* _____ _____ (i.e. wearing a specific mask) *that helps me to regain control.*

How does it make you feel to know that God wants you to give Him complete control of your life? Have you given God control of a situation before?

Day Two: Powerlessness and Defeat

[Step One]

~

God does hear us when we're broken.

Father, I thought I could do everything, but now I see I can't do any-thing. I've been knocked down, beat up, dragged around. I'm broken. What do I do now? I'm dying. The pieces are scattered all around. Father, will you pick up the pieces? I surrender. I'm defeated. I'm ready for you to mold me into the person You want me to be. Put my life back together. I'm ashamed to tell You that I can't do it by myself. I guess I never could. I see that it is You that can give me strength to fight. I am weak, Father, I'm confessing to You now. I want You to take over my life.

Do you feel this way? If you want to heal, it is imperative to decide exactly who will be in the driver's seat. Is it going to be you or God? Will you be moving in the flesh or be empowered by the Holy Spirit?

This is where your battle may begin. Ask God to help you relinquish control. Trust Him completely with your life. If you allow Him to take control, you can be assured of life and bless-ings. Remember, it's the Lord's battle! "Do not be afraid or dis-couraged—For the battle is not yours, but God's" (2 Chronicles 20:15).

☑ Take some quiet time to meditate on this verse.

Jennifer said, "Despite all the pain that food addiction has brought into my life, I still associate it with comfort and pleasure.

It's an escape from my feelings. I don't think about the long-term consequences, only about the immediate relief that food brings. Surrender, I want to so much, but I don't think I can."

Villagers that live in the forests and mountains of India catch monkeys by carving pots with necks as long as a monkey's arm and a base large enough for a banana. The monkeys can't wait to retrieve their prize. They put their arms down the neck of the jar until they have the banana tightly grasped. However, they can't pull it through the narrow neck. So they sit holding their prize tightly for fear of losing it. Eventually, the monkey becomes immobilized, and they're simple pickings for the villagers.

What are you afraid of letting go of?

I think we all are afraid of something, and that is why we are easily controlled by others; whether it's someone else's will, or media messages, or we just mindlessly follow the crowd. Sam and Adele Hooker wrote,

Our fears, our self-possessiveness, our self-protection, all the *self-things* we hold onto, cause a struggle when we're faced with giving every part of ourselves to God. Jesus wrestled in the Garden of Gethsemane until his sweat turned to blood. Finally, he and the Holy Spirit wrestled down his fleshly self will to where he could say to the Father, "Not my will but thine be done" (Matthew 26:39).[34]

Now is the time to let our faith in Jesus take over. Romans 12:1 says, "Therefore, I urge you, brothers, in view of God's mercy, to offer your bodies as living sacrifices, holy and pleasing to God—which is your spiritual worship." *Let go.*

"The will to win is important, but the will to prepare is vital."

– Joe Paterno

I Quit!

When I was a kid, my younger brothers would tickle me, or worse, pull my hair. They tickled or pulled so hard that I cried, "Stop! Stop! I surrender!" Our issues with food are like that tickler who inflicts pain and discomfort. But the difference is we have created this pain and discomfort ourselves, and the results have been far more damaging.

Are you ready to cry, "Stop! I quit!"? Plead with the Lord for release. Managing our own lives has been one big failure, and now we have to admit we cannot manage our lives any more. Once we admit our powerlessness (an emotional acceptance at the gut level), a door opens to the solution to our problem.

It is understanding *and believing* that apart from God, we can do nothing. There are many Bible characters that felt this same powerlessness, Isaiah (Isaiah 38:12–13) and Paul (Romans 7:15–20), for example. The good news is there is hope for powerlessness.

"The righteous cry out, and the Lord hears them; he delivers them from all their troubles. The Lord is close to the brokenhearted and saves those who are crushed in spirit" (Psalms 34:17–18). There is hope for you.

Reflective Questions

Describe how you are obsessed with, or addicted to, food and/or your appearance.

What are the consequences of your self-destructive habits?

What other things are you doing to avoid thinking about the pain and hurts in your life?

Day Three: The Answer
[Step Two]

~

God accomplishes our surrender.

You may be saying, "Absolute surrender implies so much! I have had so much pain and suffering. There is so much of my self-will remaining. I can't entirely give it up because I know it will cause too much trouble and agony." I come with a message to those who are fearful and anxious. God does not ask you to surrender in your strength or by the power of your will; God is willing to work it *in* you.

Look at Abraham in the Old Testament. Do you think it was by accident that God found him—the father of the faithful and the friend of God? Do you think that it was Abraham himself, apart from God, who had such faith and such obedience and such devotion? No. God raised him up and prepared him as an instrument for His glory.

God told Moses to tell Pharaoh, "But I have raised you up *(spared you)* for this very purpose, that I might show you my power and that my name might be proclaimed in all the earth" (Exodus 9:16). If God said that of him, will God not say it of you?

☑ Pray: *Father God, I am willing that You should make me willing. If there is anything holding you back or any sacrifice you are afraid of making, come to God now and prove how gracious your God is. God comes and offers to work this absolute surrender in you!*

Up to now, believing in God did not always mean we accepted His power. As Christians, we know God but do not necessarily invite Him into our lives. Jesus said in John 14:26 that the Holy Spirit would be sent in His name to teach us and remind us of all He has said. Our situation is not hopeless. Our hope lies outside of us. *Jesus is the answer.* Proverbs 16:3 tells us to commit to the Lord whatever we do, and our plans will succeed.

God leads us to victory over the trials of this life, so that we can experience success through His strength. That success comes through faith and trust. Faith isn't earned or intellectualized. Faith is a precious gift from God. *It isn't an option. It's a must.*

"A woman is like a tea bag—only in hot water do you realize how strong she is."

–Nancy Reagan

Turbulent waters are ahead on the road to healing. God knows that, and He prepares us by placing faith in our hearts. We shall never succeed in knowing ourselves until we seek to know God. Where does our competence to know ourselves come from?

2 Corinthians 3:5 says, "Not that we are competent in ourselves to claim anything for ourselves, but our competence comes from God." If we trust Him, our Lord will lead us out of the pit *when we recognize* the dysfunction in our lives. Trust. Faith. Yes, this is hard if we have been let down time after time. It is easy to forget that God has a plan when we focus daily on our hurts. Our focus must change.

Focus on the Outcome

Jesus predicted His death, "The hour has come for the Son of Man to be glorified" (John 12:23). I don't know if I would call Jesus' suffering "glorious." He knew everything about the agony that He was about to face. He also knew that three days after His crucifixion, He would leave that dark, cold tomb and rise from the dead. He knew He would see His beloved disciples again. He knew that someday, He would present those He redeemed (you and me) to His Father.

Jesus was incredible. In the midst of His suffering, what kind of perspective did Jesus keep? Hebrews 12:2: "Let us fix our eyes on Jesus, the author and perfecter of our faith, who for the joy set before him endured the cross, scorning its shame, and sat down at the right hand of the throne of God."

The writer of Hebrews says that for the "joy set before him," Jesus endured the cross. Jesus could look past the misery of the present moment to what the future outcome was going to be. What is the difference between Jesus and us?

Jesus focused on the end result rather than the painful process. Right now, many of us are losing the battle. All we can think about is stopping the pain, stopping the behavior *today*. How can you successfully focus on the outcome?

One way we can be encouraged is to look to someone who has successfully healed (recovered). I have successfully recovered from bulimia and alcohol abuse. However, I am *not* the hero. Jesus is the Hero. I focused my eyes on Jesus. As your battle to reclaim your life moves ahead, focus on Jesus and the ultimate outcome. You can have peace and strength—the kind that comes from doing His will and putting on His armor.

Reflective Questions

How do you think your battle with food compares to what Jesus faced? How will you find the courage to go on and fight?

List any roadblocks you have to trusting God and go to your prayer closet with them.

Day Four: Acceptance

~

Progress comes at the cost of leaving the old behind.

Healing requires us to understand our past, but it never asks us to live or dwell in it. God wants us to move on with our renewed lives. Now, we come to acceptance. *Acceptance is a key to healing.* I am not talking about winning the approval of man, but submitting to our Lord.

What Must You Accept to be Healed by the Lord?

Accept God and His sovereignty. God is totally and completely in charge. Period. If God is not aware of what is going to happen to us, then how can He work all things together for our good? One of God's primary attributes is love. He loves us no matter what we are like or what we have done. God's love draws us close to Him. He is the initiator. He tells us in Jeremiah 31:3 that He loves us with an everlasting love: "I have drawn you with loving-kindness." Can you accept God's character and sovereignty?

Accept God's gift of grace. It is by grace that we are saved (our faith). Grace is a gift from God, never a result of works. His promise of grace takes away our sins, and He puts His Spirit within us. This spirit enables us to live a righteous, healthy life.

When we accept God's grace, we accept that Jesus is God, the One who delivers us from sin. We acknowledge that He says who He is, and He, therefore, has the right to manage our life. Many

Christian counselors will tell you that this is essential to healing. And grace deters bitterness. The writer of Hebrews 12:15–16 said, "See to it that no one misses the grace of God and that no bitter root grows up to cause trouble and defile many." In the middle of our trials and temptations, we can be sure that God's grace is sufficient to allow us to handle anything that comes our way.

If we fail to accept these truths and fail to live in obedience, then we fall short of the grace of God. Paul never allowed his sins or unattractive appearance and speech keep him from growing and bearing fruit for Jesus. Paul accepted God's grace and could say, "Whatever I am now is all because God poured out such kindness and grace upon me" (1 Corinthians 15:10).

Will you accept God's grace in faith? We can be free of this nasty obsession if we just accept His grace and let Him do the rest.

Accept God's healing love. Love is medicine for pain. Love heals.

☑ Go to the Lord and ask Him to show you if you are failing in any of these areas. Write in your journal what God shows you and what you need to do about it.

Accepting Our Circumstances

I was guilty of blaming my circumstances for who I was and what I did. Acceptance also means accepting all circumstances, even the disastrous ones. It's our relationship with God that can help us accept and grow from experiences that seem impossible to cope with.

We all have known people who've handled disasters far more easily than we have. How did they do it? They probably asked God to help them accept and understand uncontrollable circumstances. Once God helps us accept our anger, grief, or disappointment, we're free to move on. We have choices. We can develop acceptance of any circumstance.

The apostle Paul lived with a "thorn." Whatever plagued him was a painful, ongoing trial. He even said, "Since I know it is all for Christ's good, I am quite happy about 'the thorn,' and about insults and hardships, persecutions and difficulties; for when I am weak, then I am strong—the less I have, the more I depend on him" (2 Corinthians 12:10, TLB).

When I'm worrying over some circumstance, I seek comfort in the words of Paul and God. When I am the weakest and most desperate, God works my circumstance, or myself, into something good. Our success comes through our reliance and obedience on God to direct us.

Will you shut God out or let His power fill your thorn-formed wound? Someone once said, "Time heals all wounds, unless you pick at them." God longs for us to give our wounds to Him. Ask God today to remove your thorn (and don't pick at it anymore!). Talk to Him about your struggles. Ask for His help in letting go so you can let Him take over.

> "People can meet superficial needs. But only God can meet our deep needs."
>
> –Forrester Barrington

Reflective Questions

Have you ever lost faith (or trust) in God? Describe the situation. Looking at that situation and based on what you know now about God, can you trust Him with your restoration? Explain.

Do you believe that God can redirect your self-destructive behavior? Today, do you believe God is speaking to you through your weaknesses? How?

In what ways do you need God to restore you at this moment?

Day Five: Absolute Surrender

[Step Three]

~

Do you want to get well?

In John 5:6, when Jesus saw the invalid lying there and learned he had been in this condition for a long time, He asked him, "Do you want to get well?" If Jesus said that to you, how would you respond? Are you finally ready to break the bondage?

It's time to make a decision. Are you ready to let God be totally in charge of your life? As you look at everything you've lost because of disorder eating (health, friends, respect for yourself), God's guidance is easier to accept now, isn't it?

The book of Joshua tells how the Israelites conquered their enemies in the Promised Land and divided it up among the Twelve Tribes. As long as the people relied on God and followed His will, they were victorious. Joshua 23:5 says, "The Lord your God himself will drive them out of your way. He will push them out before you, and you will take possession of their land, as the Lord your God promised you." This verse shows us that we can trust God for victory! Halleluiah!

Surrender

The time has come to turn completely your future over to the Lord. *Absolutely surrender.* We will fall and make mistakes, but when we do, we fall into the arms of God. Then we get up again. Did you know a baby falls an average of 750 times before he or she can finally stand and walk?

Scared? Unsure? Jesus provides encouragement.

> [12] *I tell you the truth, anyone who has faith in me will do what I have been doing. He will do even greater things than these, because I am going to the Father.* [13] *And I will do whatever you ask in my name, so that the Son may bring glory to the Father.* [14] *You may ask me for anything in my name, and I will do it (John 14:12–14).*

What do you want to ask Jesus for? Ask Him now in a prayer. Someone once said, "Surrendering to Jesus is the first step of an endless adventure with Him."[35]

"It's never too late to be what you might have been."
—George Eliot

Developing Humility

Let's consider how well the present management of our life is going. We consider our needs, God's ability, the future, and we take time to contemplate the changes. Finally, we make a decision that God is the only one able to manage our lives. His will for us is best. I can testify that a surrendered will is the most productive and joyful way to live.

David asks God in Psalm 143:10–11 to teach him to do God's will. The Bible tells us, "God is able and willing to do immeasurably more, even beyond all we can ask or think" (Ephesians 3:20). Think about that!

Our human will must submit to a greater will, to the will of God (as we understand God). *This is humility.* Humility is not the same as humiliation, although it often feels like humiliation to our inflated egos.

When we let go of our pride and humble ourselves, we are respected by God: "This is the one I esteem: he who is humble and contrite in spirit, and trembles at my word" (Isaiah 66:2).

Whatever we face, we are not alone. We are united with God

through Christ, whose love always triumphs over evil. Think about the difference between a life run on self-will and a life that follows God's will.

Reflective Questions

How well has self-will served you to this point? What is a recent example in your life of exercising self-will rather than following what you believe might be God's will?

Which parts of your life are you willing to turn over to God today? What prevents you from giving them up? Which parts of your life are you *not* willing to turn over to God today? Why?

☑ Write an affirmation in which you state your decision to turn this situation over to God. For example, I am no longer willing to obsess over my weight. I decide now to turn my anxiety, my concerns, and my need for security over to God.

Finale: Week Seven

~

We must remember that God knows our future.

He has our concerns and best interests at heart. Any life run on self-will can hardly be successful. The self-centeredness of our need for food and compulsive behavior has brought little or no lasting pleasure. Humility means, "The quality or condition of being humble." Humble means, "Marked by meekness or modesty in behavior, attitude, or spirit—not arrogant or prideful, or showing deferential or submissive respect, such as a humble apology."[36]

In other words, it means understanding that while we make decisions about the actions of our lives, we do not make decisions about the results of those actions. *God determines the results.* We may not understand His reasoning, but as we continue to walk by faith, we will learn His answers.

When we turn our burdens and life over to God, we are able to experience what Paul taught, "*The peace of God, which transcends all understanding, will guard* your hearts and your minds in Christ Jesus" (Philippians 4:7).

Take each step, obey, and fear not. One day, one moment at a time, is all Jesus asks. When troubles come, look to Him. He'll show you the best way to go because He has already walked the path.

Promise to Claim: "And we know that in all things God works for the good of those who love him, who have been called according to his purpose" (Romans 8:28).

I Want More Bible Food!
Week Seven: Peace With God

~

2 Chronicles 32

☑ What is easier to trust, something you can see or cannot see? Yes, something we can see, touch, feel, hear, and smell is easier to trust.

When we have problems like illness, we seek medicine. If we need to buy groceries, we get some money. If we're attacked, we call a policeman.

When Hezekiah, king of Judah, saw that Jerusalem was going to be invaded by Sennacherib, the king of Assyria, he made all the necessary preparations to ward off the invasion. "He worked hard repairing all the broken sections of the wall and building towers on it. He built another wall outside that one and reinforced the supporting terraces of the City of David. He also made large numbers of weapons and shields" (2 Chronicles 32:1–5).

Hezekiah also knew he had to prepare the hearts of the people and keep their morale up. Hezekiah appointed military officers over the people. He assembled them in the square at the city gate and encouraged them: "Be strong and courageous. Do not be afraid or discouraged because of the king of Assyria and the vast army with him, for there is a greater power with us than with him" (2 Chronicles 32:6–7).

While Hezekiah was preparing, his enemy Sennacherib, was taunting the people of Jerusalem by saying,

¹³ Do you not know what I and my fathers have done to all the peoples of the other lands? Were the gods of those nations ever able to deliver their land from my hand? ¹⁴ Who of all the gods of these nations that my fathers destroyed has been able to save his people from me? How then can your god deliver you from my hand? ¹⁵ Now do not let Hezekiah deceive you and mislead you like this. Do not believe him, for no god of any nation or kingdom has been able to deliver his people from my hand or the hand of my fathers. How much less will your god deliver you from my hand! (2 Chronicles 32:13–15)

Without minimizing the situation, Hezekiah urged his leaders to take into account the invisible, a power greater than that of Sennacherib. Not the "arm of the flesh," but the Lord their God.

What was the outcome? 2 Chronicles 32:20–23

_____

_____

_____

The invisible God fought for His people. He sent an angel who annihilated all the forces of the Assyrian king. Sennacherib had to withdraw to his own land in disgrace and then was killed by his own sons.

How can you apply this story to your life today?

_____

_____

_____

Regardless of our past struggles, we must realize that God's power, not our own, ensures our success. Be "strong and courageous," God says. Don't let circumstances get you down or discourage you. A greater power is with you. "With him is only the arm of flesh, but with us is the Lord our God to help us and to fight our battles. And the people gained confidence from what Hezekiah the king of Judah said" (2 Chronicles 32:8).

I'm Beautiful, Why Can't I See It? | 173

Week Eight: Adventure of Self-Discovery

~

Healing is a purification process.

First we must abstain from our "drug of choice"—misuse of food. We have a whole other set of challenges facing us. Unlike the alcoholic, who can abstain from alcohol, we must consume food in order to survive. This is a long-term purification process, and it continues as our souls are purged (this is a positive purging) of our deficiencies, destructive thought and behavior patterns, and negative attitudes.

As we allow God to do His work of changing us, He will purify our spirit compassionately through whatever fire or cleansing water He feels is needed. It has been said that *pain is not in the change but in the resistance to the change.* Try to relax and enjoy the purification process. Our life is made up of change. When we resist change, we resist life itself.

It's time to put God's plan ahead of our plan.

Living with our obsessions occurs in the dark. We use the darkness to hide our secrets, our hurts, our faults, our fears, our failures, and our flaws. God wants us to come out of the dark into daylight. When we enter daylight, we bring all of our deficiencies out into the open and admit who we really are.

This requires not only courage but also the ability to be authentic and real. It means facing our fear of exposure, rejection, and being hurt all over again. It's the only way to heal and stop the cycle (emotional healing), as well as grow spiritually.

> All our efficiency without His sufficiency is only a deficiency.
> —Vance Havner [37]

Day One: The Journey Begins
[Step Four]

~

Joshua, successor to Moses, had to complete the job of bringing the Israelites to the Promised Land. Because Joshua accepted God's promise and depended on God for guidance, Joshua was successful.

In Joshua 7, God made a promise to Joshua and the Hebrews. He said that as long as they were strong and courageous and followed His orders, God would give them victory in battle. Then Joshua discovered that one man, Achan, had sinned against the Lord. He had hidden items in his tent against God's command.

Joshua 7:20–21:

> [20] *Achan replied, "It is true! I have sinned against the Lord, the God of Israel. This is what I have done:* [21] *When I saw in the plunder a beautiful robe from Babylonia, two hundred shekels of silver and a wedge of gold weighing fifty shekels, I coveted them and took them. They are hidden in the ground inside my tent, with the silver underneath."*

In your life, what correlation do you see to Joshua? To Achan? Like Joshua, we know in our hearts God's promise to us, but we can't see it actually working in our life. Like Achan, we've been trying to hide and cover up things like a secret food habit or negative attitude.

☑ Open your heart and in prayer ask God to help you peel back the layers and help you face head-on those things you're hiding.

Joshua 7:25–26 says,

> [25] *Joshua said, "Why have you brought this trouble on us? The Lord will bring trouble on you today." Then all Israel stoned him, and after they had stoned the rest, they burned them.* [26] *Over Achan they heaped up a large pile of rocks, which remains to this day. Then the Lord turned from his fierce anger. Therefore that place has been called the Valley of Achor (achor means trouble) ever since.*

Once Joshua dealt with Achan, the seed of defeat was exposed and God gave Israel victory over Ai.

We can learn from Joshua. If we follow God's orders, expose all the secrets, lies, and habits, we will find victory! A. Philip Parham said, "We never know all we need to know. Self-discovery is an adventure into an ongoing mystery. God is our problem and our solution and there is nothing simple and neat about him. But he is always on the side of truth."[38] Our journey into self-discovery has begun . . .

> "A smooth sea never made a skilled mariner."
> –English Proverb

Reflective Question

Look at your support system, who is there for you day after day? Night after night? Make a list of those persons in your journal.

I hope God was at the top of your list. Perhaps He was the only one on your list. As you begin your journey of self-discovery, run to God's stronghold of acceptance. Perhaps you have rejected Him in the past and feel unworthy to take God up on His offer. Maybe you feel condemned because of your past. God will *always* be close to you and available to mend your broken spirit.

Psalms 34:18: "The Lord is close to the brokenhearted and

saves those who are crushed in spirit." Who can relieve our symptoms and lead us to a new life?

For those who serve God, He will redeem them; everyone who takes refuge in Him will be freely pardoned.

We must work to set aside our negative emotions and behaviors and believe that God will give us sufficient strength to meet our needs.

Reflective Question

List the ways that are you are benefiting now from God's presence in your life?

Day Two: Personal Examination (Part 1)
[Step Four]

～

The "Seven Deadly Sins"[39]

Pride refers to things that satisfy a person's inner longing for value or esteem. It is an excessive belief in one's own abilities, like self-importance. Pride interferes with our recognition of the grace of God. It has been called the sin from which all others arise, such as selfishness, criticism, insensitivity, self-justification, and vanity.

Envy is the desire for others' traits, status, abilities, or situation. It can also be labeled as self-pity, self-condemnation, or jealousy.

Gluttony is an inordinate desire to consume more than one person requires.

Lust is anything that someone uses to satisfy desires of the flesh. For example, an inordinate craving for the pleasures of the body or an insatiable desire for food or chemical substances.

Anger is manifested in the individual who rejects love and opts instead for fury. It is also known as resentment, hate, wrath, or bitterness.

Greed, or covetousness, is the desire for material wealth or gain.

Sloth is the avoidance of physical or spiritual work. Sloth is also laziness and procrastination.

Double-O-U-C-H! Everyone has a propensity toward the seven deadly sins. Then Satan comes along and entices us to go beyond the boundaries that God has established, and we act on those sins (or lies). Our journey requires that we examine our behavior and expand our understanding. We have brought on our own problems and need to take responsibility, for God holds us accountable.

The goal is to get in touch with our *real* selves, that part of us that we have hidden away for so long (our negative core beliefs). Unless we make a strenuous effort to face, and be rid of, all the destructive and negative things within ourselves, our decision to turn our will and our lives over to the care of God will have little meaning.

The 12-step program calls this a "moral inventory" because it concerns our behavior. I call it our "immoral inventory" because it includes the seven deadly sins and behaviors such as lying, fear, negative thinking, dishonesty, impatience, and gossiping. We need to take our own inventory to get out of this stuck place, to look at patterns and see what's going on. Looking at our own behaviors finally gives us the freedom to live our lives the way God intended us to.

Our inventory requires us to settle the past not only as we move forward, but also as we continue to follow our new way of life. This means *complete honesty* about who and what we really are—our character. We can't tap dance around our food issues in order to evade responsibility. We need deep, spiritual changes. We will benefit in proportion to the amount of honesty we bring to our inventory. If it's searching and fearless, the results will be far-reaching and substantial.

Crucify Our Sinful Nature

This can be very difficult because it's hard to be honest with ourselves. Help is available. God is willing to help us get honest with ourselves. Until we do so, we can't grow spiritually. Galatians 6:3–5 gives us a dose of medicine about our nature and pride: "If anyone thinks he is something when he is nothing, he deceives himself. Each one should test his own actions. Then he can take pride in himself, without comparing himself to somebody else, for each one should carry his own load."

Have you heard the phrase "crucify the sinful nature?" If so, what does it mean to you?

 ²² But the fruit of the Spirit is love, joy, peace, patience, kindness, goodness, faithfulness, ²³ gentleness and self-control. Against such things there is no law. ²⁴ Those who belong to Christ Jesus have crucified the sinful nature with its passions and desires. ²⁵ Since we live by the Spirit, let us keep in step with the Spirit. ²⁶ Let us not become conceited, provoking and envying each other (Galatians 5:22–26).

When we *crucify our sinful nature,* we commit to work constantly at identifying our character deficiencies (faults, blemishes, shortcomings, sins). We begin our pursuit for righteousness—the things that are pleasing to God—and we ask God to help us get rid of the deficiencies. The result is a life of love, joy, peace, and other "fruits of the spirit." I can tell you first-hand, this is a great life!

As the Holy Spirits begins to reside and work within us, He redirects all the deficiencies toward healthy, positive, and life-affirming activities.

> "Happiness consists of a solid faith, good health, and a bad memory."
>
> –Clare Boothe Luce

"Let us examine our ways and test them, and let us return to the Lord" (Lamentations 3:40). God opens our eyes to the weaknesses in our lives that need changing and helps us to build on our strengths. Personal examination of our lives will give us insight into the ways in which we have turned away from God and become self-destructive. Denial has been the operative word in our life.

Jesus acts as our advocate with the Father because of all that He went through here on earth. He is the one who can show you how to accomplish this, how to turn from denial, and how to face the truth, allowing you to move forward in your life.

☑ Write a prayer asking God for courage to face issues protected by denial.

Reflective Questions

What do you fear by having your sinful nature and character deficiencies removed?

How has sin caused you problems in the past, and what problems are you experiencing today?

Day Three: Personal Examination (Part 2)

~

Begin to walk down each aisle of your life.

Note areas of strength and weakness. When you come to relationships, take note of resentments and grudges, but also examine the healthy and loving relationships. Note all of the negative and all of the positive ways you communicate and share with others.

☑ In your journal, write (1) your immoral inventory list from the Day Two discussion, and (2) your good qualities (like persistence, organization). Don't be in a hurry to finish. This should be done prayerfully and take a significant amount of time.

Look to God for guidance so you can leave each wound at the cross. We want to find out what it is about ourselves that we need to throw out (to change) to have a more serene and productive life. To achieve that goal, we have to examine our lives to date and the negative characteristics that have caused us so much pain, as well as our assets.

1. What character deficiencies have surfaced? I.e., fear of abandonment or authority figures, control, approval seeking, obsessive/compulsive behavior, rescuing, excessive responsibility, unexpressed feelings.
2. What is your major strength? How does it support you?
3. What is your major weakness? How does it hurt you?

4. Which part of your present behavior is most damaging to your life? Explain.

5. Include the people you have hurt by your conduct (defects).

Pray Psalm 139:23–24: "Search me, O God, and know my heart; test me and know my anxious thoughts. See if there is any offensive way in me, and lead me in the way everlasting." It is important that we ask God to be part of our self-discovery process.

> "If the Son sets you free, you will be free indeed"
>
> (John 8:36).

That was a painful activity, wasn't it? It should have made you aware of many truths. You can see some things about yourself that you didn't see or acknowledge before. If you were honest and thorough with your list, you have built the foundation for healing. In other words, the first step towards rebuilding your life.

The Purification Process

If you're like me, you spring clean every year. I open all of the windows and closets to vent out the winter smell and clean each dusty corner. Sort of like our life. Shameful secrets, embarrassing behaviors, lost hope—all hidden from view.

The air of our life is musty. We've been afraid to open the doors and windows to anyone because we may be found out, rejected, and shamed. It's time to clean. That scares some of us, and for others, you can't wait to be free of the mess. *This is a purification process and an exercise in humility.*

☑ Ask the Lord to reveal any secret corners or private closets that you have never fully yielded to Him.

Day Four: Humility and Healing

[Step Five]

~

Exercising humility.

We are required to engage in an honest confrontation by admitting our faults to God, to ourselves, and to another person. OUCH! *We have to do this.* Proverbs 28:13 says, "He who conceals his sins does not prosper, but whoever confesses and renounces them finds mercy."

By confessing, we begin the important phase of setting aside our pride so that we can see ourselves truthfully. Bearing the burden of our transgressions drains us of vital energy. Confession will renew our energy level and existence. *You are free to work with anyone you please.*

That final admission to another person makes our deficiencies more real and more painful. But admission removes the power. The objective is to come out of this exercise *humbled and freed.* Consider the person you choose a blessing from God to you.

Why open up to another person? Proverbs 27:5–6 gives us the answer: "Better is open rebuke than hidden love. Wounds from a friend can be trusted, but an enemy multiplies kisses."

This is an ego-deflating experience—believe me, I know! Yet, the humility that comes from confiding our deficiencies to another person is one of the greatest rewards in healing. Humility says, "God, I need your grace! I'll do my best, but the outcome is up to you alone." Thank God for your friend who helps you see your mistakes and won't give up on you (because that friend knows and accepts that you are not perfect).

Jeremiah 14:20 says, "O Lord, we acknowledge our wickedness and the guilt of our fathers; we have indeed sinned against you." By focusing on God, we become aware of our desire to move from the bad and toward the good.

James 5:16 tells us how to move forward: "Therefore confess your sins to each other and pray for each other so that you may be healed. The prayer of a righteousness man is powerful and effective."

Prayerful sharing with a brother or sister in Christ prepares the way for healing to begin. Are you too ashamed to confess your behavior? Are you fearful of humiliation? That would not be unusual. God makes you a promise, "Do not be afraid; you will not suffer shame. Do not fear disgrace; you will not be humiliated" (Isaiah 54:4–8).

Satan will tell you that you have much to be ashamed of. He'll tell you that you will humiliate yourself by telling another. Remember, you have the authority to tell Satan he is a liar. It is written . . . *Isaiah 54* . . . this is God's promise to me!

"When I am afraid, I will trust in you. In God, whose word I praise, in God I trust; I will not be afraid. What can mortal man do to me?" (Psalms 56:3–4)

Rigorous Honesty

The goal of this exercise is to search for patterns of thinking and behavior that have served us badly. It is an examination of our lives in the loving presence of God. "He who conceals his sins *(wrongdoings)* does not prosper, but whoever confesses and renounces them finds mercy" (Proverbs 28:13).

We admit our sins to God (and to ourselves). That initiates the restoration of our personal integrity by removing our masks. How will you respond?

⁹*If we claim to be without sin, we deceive ourselves and the truth is not in us. ⁹ If we confess our sins, he is faithful and just and will forgive us our sins and purify us from all unrighteousness. ¹⁰ If we claim we have not sinned, we make him out to be a liar and his word has no place in our lives (1 John 1:8–10).*

Self-deception is human nature. Now we are challenged to be honest.

☑ Schedule an undistracted time with God and bring your list to Him. Ask God for help. Remember God knows everything. He can give us the courage to be brutally honest about ourselves. When we realize how far we have fallen, we clearly see the extent of our sin, perhaps for the first time.

Romans 3:23 says, "For all have sinned and fall short of the glory of God." The work we are doing makes us realize how we have fallen short of God's plan for us. But there is great news. The slate is wiped clean. What happened in the past *is the past!* Praise God!

Day Five: Commitment to God

[Step Six]

~

Ahh . . . the hard part is over!

Not so fast . . . there is more work ahead . . . but the best work is yet to come! The changes that are about to take place in our lives require a cooperative effort. God provides the direction and plants the desire. We must become ready for God's deepest work. Our doubts are overcome by our growing faith in what we know to be true—that God, our heavenly Father, will never leave us or forsake us (James 1:5–6).

A Time to Plant

I live in the country and watch the farmers. When a farmer works a field, he begins by preparing the soil. Then he'll sow, disc, harrow, fertilize, harrow again, and finally plant. It is a lot of work. After he plants, he stops for a while to allow the seeds time to grow. He waits and hopes for a rich crop.

God has just planted numerous seeds in our soul. The seeds of change need some time to germinate and grow. Our emotions need time to catch up with all of this. We have been plowed and prepared, and now, we give God's power the necessary time to create in us an internal change. The author of Ecclesiastes wrote:

⁹ What does the worker gain from his toil? ¹⁰ I have seen the burden

God has laid on men. [11] He has made everything beautiful in its time. He has also set eternity in the hearts of men; yet they cannot fathom what God has done from beginning to end. [12] I know that there is nothing better for men than to be happy and do good while they live. [13] That everyone may eat and drink, and find satisfaction in all his toil—this is the gift of God. [14] I know that everything God does will endure forever; nothing can be added to it and nothing taken from it. God does it so that men will revere him (Ecclesiastes 3:9–14).

God says He will *make everything beautiful in its time.* If we are not willing to wait, we are faced with self-will (insisting on our way). That's destructive. Waiting is an art and can be very powerful. If you can wait, you will often achieve something that you may not have achieved otherwise.

1 Peter 1:13 prepares us for what's ahead: "Therefore prepare your minds for actions; be self-controlled; set your hope fully on the grace to be given you when Jesus Christ is revealed." Focusing on preparation for change will encourage our faith by allowing us to detach gracefully from our past.

We have a lot of negative talk, old patterns, and beliefs shoved deep down inside (at the core). We're beginning to let go of them and are replacing them with positive patterns and behavior. The principles of God's Word are the richest source for positive pattern change.

God can't change us unless we are ready, willing, and able for Him to do so. Who among us is entirely ready to have our sin and character deficiencies removed? You may discover that there is a point at which you say, "No, I can't give this up yet." That is not uncommon. *We cannot remove sin or our character deficiencies without the help of God.*

> "I have held many things in my hands and lost them all; but whatever I have placed in God's hands, that I still possess."
>
> –Martin Luther[40]

Renewing Our Minds

[Step Seven]

Romans 12:2 reminds us not to allow the world to squeeze us into its mold, but let God remold our minds from within. As our minds turn from things of this world to things of God, our transformation begins, requiring humility. By practicing humility, we receive the grace necessary to achieve results. Now, we come to terms with our inadequacies and humbly seek God's will.

Ask yourself, "What am I allowing to mold my mind—the outside pressures or the inside power of the indwelling Jesus Christ?"

Humility is not thinking less of yourself; it's thinking of yourself less.

Ego, smugness, pride, envy, and jealousy destroy relationships faster than anything else does. Pride builds walls between people, and humility builds bridges. Pride blocks God's grace in our lives, which we must have in order to grow, change, heal, and help others. Pride has undesirable consequences. Humility is not putting yourself down or denying your strengths; rather, it is being honest about your weaknesses.

Reflective Question

Identify two character deficiencies or sins you are *not* ready to have removed. For example, something that gives you pleasure or provides some kind of reward?

Finale: Week Eight

~

How do you feel?

The work we've done has started the process of relieving the guilt and shame that has enveloped our lives for so long. The consequences of our actions are our responsibility. Humbly ask God for guidance. *Thy will, not mine, be done. Teach me not only Your will, but how to do it.*

The temptation is to pray a general prayer and ask God to remove everything as if it were a nice, neat little package. Humbly pray for the removal of your sins and shortcomings *one at a time.* The manner and timing of the removal of sin and our character deficiencies is up to God, not us. Jesus gives us encouragement.

As we place ourselves under God's control, submit to His will, and plan for our lives, that will happen. We will soon find that once our fear lessens and we accept God's care and control, we'll begin to experience love and joy in our lives.

"Repent, then, and turn to God, so that your sins may be wiped out, that times of refreshing may come from the Lord" (Acts 3:19). Human beings are called to repent, or turn around, reorient their heart and lives and live in a radically new way in the light of the kingdom Jesus introduced into the world.

Promise to Claim: "Humble yourselves under God's mighty hand, that he may lift you up in due time. Cast all your anxiety on him because he cares for you" (1 Peter 5:6–7).

I Want More Bible Food!
Week Eight: Adventure of Self-Discovery

~

Romans 6:11–14

☑ Describe a recent time when you felt you did not have control over a situation. What was that like for you?

_____

_____

_____

_____

_____

We must recognize that while we must do the legwork of removing sin and negative defects, the ultimate removal is not by our resources, but by the grace of God (in His time). We must let God work in whatever way He sees fit. We are used to being in control. We want to do it our way right now. We have to change that mindset since we are turning our lives and wills over to the care of God.

Romans 6:11–14:

[11] *In the same way, count yourselves dead to sin but alive to God in Christ Jesus.* [12] *Therefore do not let sin reign in your mortal body so that you obey its evil desires.* [13] *Do not offer the parts of your body to sin, as instruments of wickedness, but rather offer yourselves to God, as those who have*

been brought from death to life; and offer the parts of your body to him as instruments of righteousness. **14** *For sin shall not be your master, because you are not under law, but under grace.*

Circle all the references to sin.

Cross-out the words "you" and "your" and replace with personal pronouns like "my" or "I."

How have you experienced God delivering you from the sin that once enslaved your body?

_____

_____

_____

How can you offer your body as an instrument of righteousness?

_____

_____

_____

My life for His. After we choose God as our Master, we must focus on putting our old ways behind us. Paul's words say that when we count ourselves "dead to sin but alive to God," we have the power to practice our new knowledge and turn away from our sinful, addictive desires. Temptation's hold on us is shattered by our willingness to let Christ lead us to healthy behavior.

Healing from addiction and obsessive behaviors was a moment-to-moment process for me. A process of choosing things and activities that would please God and would advance His kingdom, rejecting the outside things that would gratify my desires and make me look good.

This may seem chaotic and confusing. That is normal. We are experiencing change. God taught me that to die to myself involved exchanging my reputation for His. Then it was no longer important what others thought of me. The only thing that matters is that others see Christ in me.

Does it make a difference to you whom you please if you displease the Lord?

_____

_____

_____

Does it matter whom you displease as long as you please the Lord?

_____

_____

_____

As we begin to rely on God's presence within us, our feelings of comfort and safety will overcome this anxiety. How can we be sure? 2 Thessalonians 3:3 tells us: "But the Lord is faithful, and he will strengthen and protect you from the evil one."

Week Nine: Freedom through Forgiveness

The Lord's Prayer: "Forgive us our sins, for we also forgive everyone who sins against us" (Luke 11:2–4).

That verse is something we pray in church on Sunday rather smoothly. Do we really mean that we want God (the Almighty) to forgive us when we aren't willing to forgive those who hurt us?

Jesus had more to say about forgiveness: "For if you forgive men when they sin against you, your heavenly Father will also forgive you. But if you do not forgive men their sins, your Father will not forgive your sins" (Matthew 6:14–15).

What is forgiveness? Charles Stanley wrote,

Forgiveness refers to giving up both resentment toward someone else, and the right to get even, no matter what that person has done. Unforgiveness, then, describes a deliberate refusal to let go of ill will or your right to repay the offender in some fashion; it is based on the unChristlike attitude that somebody has to pay for the hurt, a position for which there is simply no biblical justification.[41]

Forgiveness is saying, "I'm not going to hurt anymore because of what someone else did to me." Forgiveness is a choice and a process. I knew that if I was to grow, then I had to release the hurts of my past. This meant that I had to ask God to empower me to move forward to forgive those responsible, whether they deserved it or not. Eventually I forgave all the people who hurt, teased, and rejected me.

The hardest person to forgive was myself. I hated myself for wasting so many productive years (and money) catering to the monster bulimia, years I could never get back. There were so many things I wanted to do all over.

Secondly, I asked for my mother's forgiveness. I confessed to her that I stole money from her to support my food and laxative addiction. She forgivingly said, "What you did hasn't changed the way I love and think of you. We've all done things that we aren't proud of. There isn't anyone to judge you except God. And we know how forgiving He is."

I felt the last chain and shackle fall off. It was freeing to give and receive forgiveness. Now it's your turn!

Note: This week's work is longer because forgiveness is so critical to healing. I would encourage you to try to put more time aside this week for this very important lesson.

Day One: Finding Our Way to Forgiveness
[Step Eight]

⁓

Many of us have been victims of some form of abuse.

Emotionally, physically, or verbally abused by a family member we most likely trusted and love. If there ever was a tragic victim, it was Tamar (2 Samuel 13:20). She was a beautiful, royal princess, the daughter of King David. Her life should have been a fairy tale, but it became a nightmare. Her spoiled and deceitful half-brother, Amnon, fell in love with her (1) and raped her. After he raped her, he threw her out of his room because his lust changed to hatred.

Grieving, Tamar tore her robe (a symbol of her virginity) and wept loudly. Absalom, another brother, appeared to deny Tamar her grief and discounted her emotions by saying, "Be quiet now, my sister, he is your brother. Don't take this thing to heart." Tamar lived in her brother Absalom's house a desolate woman (20).

Her father, David, was furious but did nothing. In the privacy and safety of her own home, Tamar had been violated and hurt. Those who should have defended her victimized her. Her people, her honor, her future were negated by a family that didn't respect boundaries. They didn't know love or respect. Two years later, Absalom killed Amnon for raping his sister (2 Samuel 13:32).

What happened to Tamar? What happened to her heart and her soul? Did her pain surface as depression, anger, an eating disorder, or other addiction? I wonder if she had someone to pour her heart out to. Her heart must have been full of anger, hurt, shame, and grief. Was she ever able to forgive and know the comfort of God? We don't know. But Satan probably took advantage of her injured mind and heart.

Can you feel Tamar's pain, anger, shame, and grief? I hope Tamar was able to feel the words in Psalms 71:20–21: "Though you have made me see troubles, many and bitter, you will restore my life again; from the depths of the earth you will again bring me up. You will increase my honor and comfort me once again."

Healing begins with the understanding that God is sovereign and in control. Tamar had every reason to be angry, even hate Amnon. We all have hurts, and we all have someone in our life that we're angry and resentful of; perhaps it's only ourselves.

"We achieve inner health only through forgiveness—the forgiveness not only of others but also of ourselves."

–Joshua Loth Liebman (1907–1948)

Unforgiving Spirit

Unforgiveness is guaranteed to hinder our growth because an unforgiving spirit is an evil spirit that causes devastation. It plants roots of bitterness in our heart. It's like pouring acid in us, a caustic substance that eats through our heart. Why is it so hard for us to "forgive and forget" the injuries of life? Dorothy wrote, *My mother owes me. I lost my childhood because of her neglect and drunkenness. I hate her.*

God never promised any of us freedom from pain. We can begin to find happiness if we free our mind of resentment and bitterness—put the past behind and see the process as empowering.

Matthew 18:21–35, the parable of the unmerciful servant.

²¹ *Then Peter came to Jesus and asked, "Lord, how many times*

shall I forgive my brother when he sins against me? Up to seven times?" [22] Jesus answered, "I tell you, not seven times, but seventy-seven times." [23] Therefore, the kingdom of heaven is like a king who wanted to settle accounts with his servants. [24] As he began the settlement, a man who owed him ten thousand talents was brought to him. [25] Since he was not able to pay, the master ordered that he and his wife and his children and all that he had be sold to repay the debt. [26] The servant fell on his knees before him. "Be patient with me," he begged, "and I will pay back everything." [27] The servant's master took pity on him, canceled the debt and let him go. [28] But when that servant went out, he found one of his fellow servants who owed him a hundred denarii. He grabbed him and began to choke him. "Pay back what you owe me!" he demanded. [29] His fellow servant fell to his knees and begged him, "Be patient with me, and I will pay you back." [30] But he refused. Instead, he went off and had the man thrown into prison until he could pay the debt. [31] When the other servants saw what had happened, they were greatly distressed and went and told their master everything that had happened. [32] Then the master called the servant in. "You wicked servant," he said, "I canceled all that debt of yours because you begged me to. [33] Shouldn't you have had mercy on your fellow servant just as I had on you?" [34] In anger his master turned him over to the jailers to be tortured, until he should pay back all he owed. [35] "This is how my heavenly Father will treat each of you unless you forgive your brother from your heart."

Reflective Questions

Is there a particular situation or person that comes to mind when you read this passage?

What do you think Jesus was trying to teach in this parable? What message does God have for *you* in His Son's words?

Like Dorothy and the wicked servant, you can hold that person responsible, harbor hatred, and consequently, carry feelings of anger forever. Or you can begin healing when you chose to forgive. In order to heal, we must forgive again and again—the big wrongs and the little ones. The alternative is to hold on to hatred and bitterness, which eventually will hurt all our relationships. Give yourself grace.

Sheila Walsh wrote, "In my situation, as long as I was unwilling to let go and forgive, there was still a nail in my wrist, and every time I talked to someone about the situation, it cut in a little deeper."[42] It is our responsibility to pull out that nail.

Many people won't choose to forgive. They live unhappy lives of bitterness and unforgiveness. If it was a parent who hurt them, they become that parent, in spite of the fact they swore they never would. Why do you think people who have been abused as children abuse their own children? Why do children of alcoholics become an alcoholic or marry one?

Dr. Gregory Jantz says,

If the child of the past and the adult of the present are to integrate fully into the person of the future, there comes a time when both must release the hurts of the past. This doesn't mean that you forget what has been done to you, but that you forgive those responsible, whether they deserve your forgiveness or not. Forgiveness is the final destination on your healing journey. The road that lies beyond is one of health.[43]

Reflective Questions

What is your greatest battle with forgiveness?

What lack of forgiveness or bitterness is still attached to you?

Day Two: On the Road to Forgiveness

~

I'll never forgive him as long as I live!

Many of our problems come as a result of an unforgiving attitude toward others who have offended us. I heard a story of a woman who was sexually molested over and over by her father. She became pregnant numerous times. One pregnancy was aborted, the second resulted in a child that died, and the third, a deformed child that lived. She didn't ever want anyone to touch her (who can blame her?). When she tried to tell police, her parents said she was lying. At that point, she became suicidal.

She could *not* forgive her father. That would be *really* hard, wouldn't it? What her father did makes us angry. God was angry too. This is righteous, justified anger. Once this woman realized and understood that God was angry with her father, too, the healing process began. Naturally, it took time for her to work through the process.

Years passed, and God did miraculous things in that woman because she chose to forgive her father. She now loves being a woman, and people who knew her before said you wouldn't even recognize her. She leaned on God's Word to trust Him as the Father she never knew.

Won't you do the same; forgive those you harbor unforgiveness against? When you do, you'll find your relationship with God, and others will become so much more enjoyable. People will say, "You wouldn't even recognize her now. She's 'maaav-el-ous.'"

Forgiveness is a process and a decision. Jesus stressed the urgency of reconciliation, and Paul gives us instructions: "Therefore, as God's chosen people, holy and dearly loved, clothe yourselves with compassion, kindness, humility, gentleness, and patience. Bear with each other and forgive whatever grievances you may have against one another" (Colossians 3:12–13).

Who Can Receive God's Forgiveness?

• 1 John 1:9: "If we confess our sins, he is faithful and just and will forgive us our sins and purify us from all unrighteousness."

• Acts 3:19: "Repent, then, and turn to God, so that your sins may be wiped out, that times of refreshing may come from the Lord."

• Psalms 32:5: "Then I acknowledged my sin to you and did not cover up my iniquity. I said, 'I will confess my transgressions to the Lord'—and you forgave the guilt of my sin."

"When one door of happiness closes, another opens; but often we look so long at the closed door that we do not see the one that has been opened for us."

–Helen Keller (1880–1968)

Forgiving Others When They Are Not Sorry

Kerri said, "My father did horrible things to me. He thinks he's justified and shows no remorse. How can I forgive him?" It is not uncommon to want the person that has hurt us to show some kind of remorse or confess their guilt before we forgive them. Often, that never happens.

Jesus tells us about forgiving another if they aren't sorry: "And when you stand praying, if you hold anything against anyone, forgive him, so that your Father in heaven may forgive you your sins. But if you do not forgive, neither will your Father who is in heaven forgive your sins" (Mark 11:25).

If that person has hurt you or has done something against you, Matthew 5:23–24: "Therefore, if you are offering your gift at the altar and there remember that your brother has something against you, leave your gift there in front of the altar. *First go and be reconciled to your brother; then come and offer your gift.*"

Scripture is pretty clear on the importance of forgiveness. God is the only One who can forgive our sins. We are not in a position to refuse *anyone* forgiveness because God has forgiven us.

Forgiveness Letters

List in your journal the person(s) you can't forgive. Write out why.

For each person listed, finish this sentence, *I will forgive (name) if they will* . . .

Pray and ask God to *forgive you* for the ways you have hurt others and to help *you forgive* those on your list.

☑ Get out your *angry* letter(s) from week six. Now, write another letter to this person(s). Again, complete this letter to God in your journal. This time you will release them from your unforgiveness (judgment). Or you can write out a statement(s) of forgiveness: *Dear God, I forgive (name) for* . . . [be specific]

If you are part of a group, be prepared to read one of the letters at your next meeting.

Day Three: Restoring Relationships
[Step Eight]

~

In Genesis 37, we meet Joseph, Jacob's son.

Jacob was Joseph's favorite, and all the other brothers knew it. "When his brothers saw that their father loved him more than any of them, they hated him and could not speak a kind word to him" (3–4). We follow Joseph through a series of near-tragic disasters brought about at the hands of his brothers and others.

"Come now, let's kill him and throw him into one of these cisterns and say that a ferocious animal devoured him" (20). Then his brothers sold him to a caravan of Ishmaelite slave traders heading for Egypt (25). Worst yet, the brothers got Joseph's robe, slaughtered a goat, and dipped the robe in the blood. They took the ornamented robe back to their father and said, "We found this. Examine it to see whether it is your son's robe." He recognized it and said, "It is my son's robe! Some ferocious animal has devoured him. Joseph has surely been torn to pieces" (31–34). Neither the brothers, nor Joseph's grieving father, Jacob, ever expected to see Joseph again. However, God had other plans.

Contrary to his brother's expectations, Joseph did very well in Egypt. He was given a prominent position in the house of Potiphar and was proven reliable, innovative, and hardworking. Then Potiphar's wife wanted to bed Joseph, but he refused to give into temptation. She cried rape (Genesis 39:17, TLB), and Joseph was thrown into prison.

²⁰ Joseph's master took him and put him in prison, the place where the king's prisoners were confined. But while Joseph was there in the prison, ²¹ the Lord was with him; he showed him kindness and granted him favor in the eyes of the prison warden. ²² So the warden put Joseph in charge of all those held in the prison, and he was made responsible for all that was done there. ²³ The warden paid no attention to anything under Joseph's care, because the Lord was with Joseph and gave him success in whatever he did (Genesis 39:20–23).

If I were Joseph, I would have been angry and heartbroken by my brother's betrayal, at Potiphar's wife for crying rape, and at the Lord for allowing my incarceration, when all I was doing was the honorable thing. Was Joseph angry? We don't get a glimpse into Joseph's thoughts or heart, but they had to be long, dark years. Can't you hear him say, *Lord, I chose to honor You, but You did not come to my defense. Why?* We learn that the Lord was with Joseph.

It's tempting to think that when God is with us, everything will work out perfectly. That's not the case. What is important is how we handle *our* situation. We see that no matter what happened to Joseph, he found favor with God because of how he lived. He accepted the death of his dreams and waited to fulfill God's plan for his life.

Joseph had no idea that in a few years he would be taken out of jail to interpret a dream for Pharaoh and put in charge of Egypt. He had no idea that all the years in prison were preparing him for the rest of his life. But God knew.

Shift for a moment to God's perspective—the parent. Do you think He deliberately "pulled back" to allow Joseph's faith to mature? In Chapter 45, Joseph is given the opportunity to reveal himself to his brothers. He tests them to determine if they have developed any character since they abandoned him. He said,

Then Joseph said to his brothers, "Come close to me." When they had

done so, he said, "I am your brother Joseph, the one you sold into Egypt! [5] *And now, do not be distressed and do not be angry with yourselves for selling me here, because it was to save lives that God sent me ahead of you.* [6] *For two years now there has been famine in the land, and for the next five years there will not be plowing and reaping.* [7] *But God sent me ahead of you to preserve for you a remnant on earth and to save your lives by a great deliverance. (4–7)*

Now, the tables were turned. The brothers were devastated. Egypt was the only place with grain, and Joseph was in charge of distributing it. If I were Joseph, I'd be thinking, *Why should I help them? They tried to kill me!* His brothers then came and threw themselves down before him. "We are your slaves," they said. But Joseph said to them, "Don't be afraid. Am I in the place of God? You intended to harm me, but *God intended it for good to accomplish what is now being done, the saving of many lives*" (Genesis 50:20–21). What did Joseph do? He didn't blame his brothers; he provided for them. The same lips that once begged his brothers to stop, which trembled with fear and grief, now spoke with unwavering confidence in God's plan.

What did Joseph understand about God (20) that helped him forgive his brothers? "We know that in ALL things God works for the good of those who love him" (Romans 8:28)—rejection in one's childhood, alcoholic parents, a cheating husband, or illness. No matter what life has in store for us, *God can turn anything into a blessing.* Yes, anything!

"To err is human, to forgive divine."

–Alexander Pope, poet

Reflective Questions

What about Joseph's story (God bringing good out of what appeared to be a disaster) can you apply to your life this week?

Look at your situation at this very moment. Can you say, "God intends this for good?"

Can you see that God is in control and more powerful than your enemies? Why or why not?

Day Four: Mending Fences
[Step Nine]

~

How do you feel about a heart transplant?

Before starting this study, many of us blamed others for the turmoil in our lives. Maybe you even held God responsible. It's time to release the need to blame others and accept full responsibility for our own lives. We ask forgiveness (the 12-step program calls this "making amends"), which means restoring personal relationships—mending fences. We are talking about a heart transplant, a healing change. This means letting go of that hard-heartedness, *one of the greatest blocks to our ability to give and receive love.*

Our willingness to mend the fences in our lives gives us an opportunity to love one another and experience how God lives in us. It increases our self-esteem. It may or may not benefit the other person; he or she may not be willing to put matters aside. *But we become healed.*

God does this for us if we ask. Ezekiel 11:19 says, "I will give them an undivided heart and put a new spirit in them; I will remove from them their heart of stone and give them a heart of flesh."

When I was a kid, I fought all the time with my brothers. We constantly tattled and blamed each other. Kids love to blame each other for their troubles and evade responsibility. Eventually, we grew up. Now, we grow up all over again and do what spiritually mature people do; take responsibility for our actions without consideration for hurts and wrongs done to us by others.

Forgiving Those Who Have Hurt Us

Do not judge, and you will not be judged. Do not condemn, and you will not be condemned. *Forgive, and you will be forgiven. Give, and it will be given to you.* A good measure . . . will be poured into your lap. *For with the measure you use, it will be measured to you"* (Luke 6:37–38).

Receiving the gift of God's love and *giving it to others freely* assures us of an abundant life. This is the second secret to healing! (What was the first secret? Hint: Week Three).

We forgive those who have hurt us no matter what they have done to us so that we can be free. Hate binds. Love frees.

Jesus also reminds us, "Why do you look at the speck of sawdust in your brother's eye and pay no attention to the plank in your own eye? How can you say to your brother, 'Let me take the speck out of your eye,' when all the time there is a plank in your own eye?" (Matthew 7:3–4)

Forgiveness may not come easily. Pray about it until it does. It is through forgiveness that we can finally let go of the past and begin anew.

> "Being unwilling to forgive means that we hold everyone around us to a standard of perfection—something that we ourselves will never achieve."
>
> –Gary L. Thomas[44]

Forgiveness Versus Trust

Many people are reluctant to forgive because they don't understand the difference between forgiveness and trust. Forgiveness is letting go of the past. Trust is what you do with your future behavior.

Forgiveness must be immediate, whether or not the other person asks for it. Trust must be rebuilt over time and requires developing a track record. If someone continues to hurt you, God commands you to forgive them now. But you are not commanded to trust them. They must prove they have changed over time.

Writing Your Forgiveness List

God's promise of healing cannot be fulfilled if we refuse to relinquish our anger and resentment. We begin the process by writing a forgiveness list.

Your forgiveness list should include the names of everyone you have hurt and who appeared in your inventory list (Week Eight). With God's help, think again. Have you forgotten or over-looked anyone? Reject the idea that you have hurt no one. This is a test of humility.

Example:

Person	Relationship	Nature of Harm	Sin/Defects	Effect on Others	Effect on Me	ACT OF FORGIVENESS
John	husband	angry insults	dishonest, greedy	fear, anger	guilt, shame	
Mary	co-worker	stole her snacks	grandiosity	anger, distrust	guilt, shame	

☑ Consider each person carefully and prayerfully. Look at each relationship and consider how you hurt them. Be as thorough as possible. For example, "I have stolen money from my husband to buy food. The amount of money that I've spent on food could have been used for a down payment on a house by now; I have lied to my counselor Jennie and my family about the severity and frequency of my binging and purging."

Day Five: Forgiveness in Action

~

From the organization, *Voice of the Martyrs:*[45]

Damare, a small Sudanese boy, was taken as a slave and forced to tend camels after radical Muslims attacked his village. One day, Damare, who had been raised in a Christian home, snuck away from his master to attend a church service. When he returned, his Muslim master was waiting for him and accused Damare of committing a deadly act, "meeting with infidels." He dragged Damare into a field where he nailed Damare's feet and knees into a large board while the boy cried out in agony. Damare was miraculously rescued. He said that just as Jesus was nailed and forgave, he forgives also.

What bold faith from a simple Sudanese boy! That e-mail brought tears to my eyes as I thought of all the petty grievances I imagined so horrible.

Like Damare, we are asked to complete the forgiveness process. Have you ever noticed when you put your garbage can out week after week, there is always that "gunk" stuck on the bottom that never gets discarded. It stays stuck on the bottom until you wash it out with soap and water. That's what we're doing, washing out that gunk.

Don't be scared off. The qualities we need to wash out the gunk are available from God! He can give us the judgment and careful sense of timing, courage, and stamina we need.

Don't expect to suddenly feel love for this person(s), especially if the offense was great. Forgiving and making amends does not mean that what happened to you was okay or even that you have to let that person back into your life again. You are lining up your will with God's will in simple obedience.

The Rebuilding Process

Natural disasters are always gripping news. What happens to these devastated areas after the news cameras go away? We don't see the hard work of rebuilding that takes place after the disaster. That's what we're doing; starting the rebuilding process that takes place after our hurricane blows through. It is a painfully humbling process but so rewarding.

My dad uses this quote frequently: "God helps those who help themselves." He taught me that even though God is all-powerful and the God of miracles, I still had to do my part. There are eight practical biblical steps to restoring (rebuilding) a relationship:

Pray. Take your problem to God and tell him exactly how you feel. We often find that either God changes our heart, or He changes the other person's. The apostle James noted that many of our conflicts and quarrels are caused by prayerlessness. James 4:1–2 teaches us: "What causes fights and quarrels among you? Don't they come from your desires that battle within you? You want something but don't get it. You kill and covet, but you cannot have what you want. You quarrel and fight. You do not have, because you do not ask God." God says, *Come to me first.*

Take the lead. It doesn't matter whether we are the offender or the offended; God expects us to make the first move. Jesus commanded that it even take priority over group worship. Matthew 5:23–24 tells us not to procrastinate or make excuses, as it makes matters worse. In conflict, time heals nothing; it only causes hurts to fester. Psalm 66:18 says sin (including unresolved conflict) blocks our fellowship with God and keeps our prayers from being answered (besides making us miserable).

Confess your part of the conflict. If we are serious about restoring a relationship, we begin by admitting our own mistakes (sin). We should ask an unbiased person to help evaluate our actions before meeting with the person, and ask God to show us how much of the problem is our fault. *Father, am I being unrealistic, insensitive, or too sensitive?* Honestly own up.

Be sympathetic. Paul taught that we look out for one another, not just for ourselves. We shouldn't try to talk the person out of how they feel. Just listen and let them unload. Then you say, *I value your opinion. I care about our relationship.*

Attack the problem, not the person. The Bible tells us how we are to handle confrontation. David is a good example, "I will watch my ways and keep my tongue from sin; I will put a muzzle on my mouth as long as the wicked are in my presence" (Psalms 39:1). Let's choose our words wisely. A soft answer is always better than a sarcastic one. In resolving conflict, *how* we say something, along with our body language, is as important as *what* we say (Proverbs 16:21). We are never persuasive when we are abrasive. Paul said not to use harmful words, but positive words that build up.

Cooperate. Paul also said to do everything possible to live in peace with everybody. That is positive growth toward healing. Jesus said, "Blessed are the peacemakers, for they will be called sons (daughters) of God" (Matthew 5:9).

Reconciliation, not resolution. Not everyone will agree about everything. Reconciliation focuses on the relationship, while resolution focuses on the problem. We can agree to disagree. This doesn't mean we give up finding a solution.

Use your head. In choosing *not* to make restitution, our only reason must be that it would result in harm to another person. Forgiveness related to adultery, crimes, or acts that might result in being fired from a job have the potential to harm others.

Remember, our forgiveness does not depend on them. All we can do is the right thing. How they react to our effort is a matter between them and God. If we caused anguish, then we ask ourselves how we best can make reparation (repair the damage) for it. *Some kind of reparation is required,* even if we can't completely restore the damage.

Are you willing to endure whatever consequences are necessary for you to begin making forgiveness? Forgiveness is a choice, a choice to obey God, regardless of our emotions.

Get Out Your Forgiveness List:

In your column "Forgiveness," describe the amend you intend to make to each person on the list. Go down the list person by person, and approach each person with gentleness, sensitivity, and understanding. God can help us to know the best way to make contact and restore our relationships. Pause right now and talk to God about that person(s) on your list.

Describe how you intend to make the necessary forgiveness. Can you pick up the phone and begin the process? Why or why not?

Finale: Week Nine

~

Forgiveness is a choice.

A young man was sentenced to prison for a heinous crime. His family was extremely angry with him for disgracing them and throwing his life away. Years later, he was released and wanted to go home. He wrote his family telling them his wishes. He wrote, *I know I have hurt you and you are very angry with me. You have every right to be. I have suffered, too, and am remorseful. Please forgive me. I want to come home. If you forgive me, tie a white ribbon on the big maple tree in the pasture. Then I will know you have forgiven me and I can come home.*

He rode the train, and as the train neared his family's property, he couldn't bear to see if the white ribbon was hanging on the tree. He said to the man sitting next to him, "Sir, we're coming up on my family's farm. There is a big maple tree in the pasture. Is there a white ribbon hung on it?" The passenger said, "No, there isn't one white ribbon." He paused. "There are dozens of white ribbons in all the trees. In fact, there are white ribbons all over— on the clothesline, the fences, and the front porch." The young man's eyes filled with tears, "I've been forgiven! I'm home!"

Too often we say, "Just forgive and forget," which masks, rather than heals. It's time to acknowledge the very issues that exist, to deal with the past, and to chart new relationships based on acceptance and forgiveness.

Forgiveness is medicine for pain. It heals the hole in our heart, the unpleasant memories, the seething rage, resentment, and the ferocity of hate. To obey God and forgive is to say, "God, I love you, and I am willing to sacrifice myself and desires."

Promise to Claim: "Be kind and compassionate to one another, forgiving each other, just as in Christ God forgave you" (Ephesians 4:32).

I Want More Bible Food!
Week Nine: Freedom through Forgiveness

~

Acts 7:54–60

☑ Describe a time you felt crucified.

Forgiveness is the key. Other sins can be present, and if your heart condemns you for something else, then, of course, you do not have confidence before God. But it is lack of forgiveness that most often comes between people and God.

Read Acts 7:54–60: The Stoning of Stephen.

Stephen was able to forgive those who stoned him. Who else was able to forgive others? What can you take away from this story?

_____

_____

_____

_____

_____

_____

_____

_____

Read Luke 23:34 and Romans 15:1–3. What do these verses teach us?

_____

_____

_____

_____

Jesus' Crucifixion

Even though you may have suffered at the hands of another person, none of us can say we have ever been crucified. Jesus underwent a horrific torture and humiliation for *our sin*. He was sinless and did nothing to deserve crucifixion.

If Jesus can forgive those who tormented, tortured, and crucified Him, can you forgive those who have tormented and tortured you? When we clearly see how much we've been forgiven, it's easier to forgive others. That is why Christ was crucified—to take on all our hurts, pain, and the insensitive people in our life—past, present and future.

As we grow in spiritual strength, we become willing servants of God, caring for our neighbors as God cares for us.

Week Ten: Healing for Life

Joy is one of God's greatest medicines.

Once we make restitution and receive God's forgiveness, our healing and restoration takes place. Joy can finally replace guilt, shame, rejection, fear, and all of those ugly emotions.

"You turned my wailing into dancing; you removed my sackcloth and clothed me with joy, that my heart may sing to you and not be silent. O Lord my God, I will give you thanks forever" (Psalm 16:11). This is David's response after he accepted God's forgiveness.

God wants the same for us. God not only wants to fill us with peace and joy, but He wants us to be so full of Him that we overflow with His joy and hope for our future (Romans 15:13).

1 Peter 1:4–8 describes being filled with an "inexpressible joy":

⁴ And God has reserved for his children the priceless gift of eternal life; it is kept in heaven for you, pure and undefiled, beyond the reach of change and decay.⁵ And God, in his mighty power, will make sure that you get there safely to receive it because you are trusting him. It will be yours in that coming last day for all to see. ⁶ So be truly glad! There is wonderful joy ahead, even though the going is rough for a while down here. ⁷ These trials are only to test your faith, to see whether or not it is strong and pure. It is being tested as fire tests gold and purifies it—and your faith is far more precious to God than mere gold; so if your faith remains strong after being tried in the test tube of fiery trials, it will bring you much praise and glory and honor on the day of his return. ⁸ You love him even though you have never seen him; though not seeing him, you trust him; and even now you are happy with the inexpressible joy that comes from heaven itself (TLB).

Peter is describing a very real feeling of joy and encouragement. This comes from knowing we don't have to endure our pain and struggles alone. God is with us, even when we can't see Him. He continues to give us courage and strength to persevere. God helps us see that our trials serve His purpose. They move us down His path toward greater faith and a healthier life. Joy brings into focus our distorted perceptions.

Even in the war zones of life, there is joy because our God is great, and we are bathed in His love. The joy Jesus gives us isn't grounded in our circumstances—it's grounded in Him. We fix our eyes on Jesus and find in Him the reason for joy.

Joy is healthy.

Joy is freeing.

Joy is contagious.

Day One: Breaking Free from Social Pressures

~

Culture. Family. Me.

Studies show that emotional eating is triggered by factors such as the culture, family influence, and how we as an individual handle growth and development. Most of us felt forced to conform to what our culture or family told us to be. Part of the restoration process is breaking free from these social pressures—the pressures to be thin and to be perfect.

The apostle Paul tells us how to be free of sociocultural influences that are contrary to God's Word:

Therefore, I urge you, brothers, in view of God's mercy, to offer your bodies as living sacrifices, holy and pleasing to God—this is your spiritual act of worship. Do not conform any longer to the pattern of this world, but be transformed by the renewing of your mind. Then you will be able to test and approve what God's will is—his good, pleasing and perfect will (Romans 12:1–2).

What do you think Paul means when he says we are to "offer our bodies to God?" Eugene Peterson's *The Message* translates this passage,

So here's what I want you to do, God helping you: Take your everyday, ordinary life—your sleeping, eating, going-to-work, and walking-around life—and place it before God as an offering. Embracing what God does for you is the best thing you can do for him. Don't become so well-adjusted to your culture that you fit into it without even thinking. Instead, fix your attention on God. You'll be changed from the inside out. Readily recognize what he wants from you, and quickly respond to it. Unlike the culture around you, always dragging you down to its level of immaturity, God brings the best out of you, develops well-formed maturity in you.

God doesn't want us to copy the behavior and customs of this world. He wants us to be a new and different person in everything we do and think. Then we learn from our own experience how His ways can ultimately satisfy us, not our self-centered ways.

> "Happiness is a by-product of a healthy attitude. And a healthy attitude is one that takes the normal turmoil of life and mixes it with a belief in God's presence."
>
> –Karen Casey[46]

Freedom

We are approaching the end of the study. I trust you have made some important strides. Before you proceed, ask yourself if, somehow, you still feel that you are *not* on the road to freedom? Maybe you've become so used to living in bondage that you are resisting freedom.

The Israelites were slaves for four hundred years. Moses was the one who came to tell them they could be free. But the Israelites were more concerned about what their masters would do that they missed what God's freedom would bring. Freedom for them meant that Pharaoh would be angry, and therefore the Egyptians would attack them. Freedom didn't seem worth the price.

The Israelites failed for three reasons, (1) they had no faith in God, (2) they lacked self-respect, and (3) they were not willing to pay the price for success (faith) and missed God's abundant blessings.

Reflective Questions

Do you feel like an Israelite? Before moving on, stop and pray. Ask God for direction. Ask Him if you need to go back and review certain chapters.

What are your plans for the areas in your life that still require God's healing power and touch?

Day Two: Victory Over Temptations and "Triggers"
(Part 1)

~

Fact: **We cannot escape temptation.**

A temptation or a trigger is an enticement by Satan that always includes sin and is aimed at bringing us down. It is the deception that something is more to be desired than God and His ways.

For example, everyday we are bombarded with hundreds of media messages, which produce thousands of thoughts—thoughts that can bring temptation (and fear) into our mind. Often, temptation equals relapse if we don't stand strong with God. But the difference is that in Christ, we have the strength to resist temptation that we never had before.

Because Jesus experienced temptation when He suffered, He is able to help us when we are tempted. When He taught the Lord's Prayer, Jesus said to pray, "And lead us not into temptation but deliver us from the evil one" (Matthew 6:13). Therefore, the prayer for deliverance from temptation is that we would not fall for that deception, but know that God and His ways are to be desired above all else.

Even with Christ in our lives, we are not immune from temptation. There will always be certain situations that make us vulnerable to temptation. Ads for diets as well as other products and services that are counterproductive to healthy living are a reality of the world we live in. Learning to "navigate" through these temptations (triggers) is part of the work.

Autobiography

I walk down the street and see the bakery. I won't go near it.
I walk down the street and see the bakery. I'll walk past it.
I will go into the bakery. I will only order coffee.
I will order coffee. I will just look at the donuts.
As I sip my coffee, I will only smell the donuts.
I will buy one donut. I will give it to my roommate.
My roommate's not home. I will just smell her donut.
Okay, I will just have a tiny taste. She won't mind.
Just one big bite. I will not eat the whole donut.
I ate the donut! She'll never know.

When did I lose the battle? I could very easily say, "That's just the way I am when it comes to food—weak," and attack that donut.

The Scriptures use Israel's history as a warning about the perils of temptation. Paul relates that despite God's abundant blessing, the nation nevertheless chose the wrong pathway. The Israelites were tempted and they yielded. In fact, that nation's entire history was a recurring cycle of obedience, blessing, temptation, and rebellion (1 Corinthians 10:1–12). That happens with us too. We repeatedly fall into the same old temptation. Hence the phrase, "The devil made me do it."

God promises us help when we encounter temptation:

• 1 Corinthians 10:13: "No temptation has seized you except what is common to man. And God is faithful; he will not let you be tempted beyond what you can bear. But when you are tempted, he will also provide a way out so that you can stand up under it."

• Titus 2:11–12: "For the grace of God that brings salvation has appeared to all men. It teaches us to say "No" to ungodliness and worldly passions, and to live self-controlled, upright, and godly lives in this present age."

He tells us what to do to overcome temptation:

• Matthew 26:41: "Watch *(be on guard)* and *pray* so that you will not fall into temptation."

• Ephesians 6:13: "Therefore *put on the full armor of God,* so that when the day of evil comes, you may be able to stand your ground, and after you have done everything, to stand."

> "A finished person is a boring person."
>
> –Anna Quindlen

Reflective Questions

Begin recording when you are most tempted to eat, binge, and/or purge. Is there a particular day of week or time of day?

Where are you most tempted? Ask, "Who is with me when I'm tempted? How do I usually feel when I'm most tempted? Is it when I'm lonely, depressed, mad at my mother or father, bored, or stressed?"

Identify patterns of temptation and be prepared to confront those situations.

Day Three: Victory over Temptation and "Triggers"
(Part 2)

~

Do we use the word "temptation" correctly?

Oswald Chambers wrote,

Temptation is not sin, it is the thing we are bound to meet if we are men *(human)*. Not to be tempted would be to be beneath contempt. Many of us, however, suffer from temptations from which we have no business to suffer, simply because we have refused to let God lift us to a higher plane where we would face temptations of another order.[47]

Some circumstances will cause you to fall immediately, while others won't bother you at all. These situations are unique to your weaknesses. You need to identify them because Satan already knows them. He is constantly working to put you into those circumstances.

Peter reveals Satan's motives, "Be self-controlled and alert. Your enemy the devil prowls around like a roaring lion looking for someone to devour. Resist him, standing firm in the faith" (1 Peter 5:8–9).

Temptation or Test?

Do you think God will ever tempt you? James 1:13: "When

tempted, no one should say, 'God is tempting me.' For God cannot be tempted by evil, nor does He tempt anyone." Satan is the tempter. Temptation's objective is to get you to do wrong, and God will never do that.

Will God ever test us? James 1:2–4: "Consider it pure joy, my brothers, whenever you face trials of many kinds, because you know that the testing of your faith develops perseverance. Perseverance must finish its work so that you may be mature and complete, not lacking anything."

God will test us, but His tests will always strengthen us. A test helps us to grow stronger and more mature. Each *test* builds that *test*imony. A test seeks to bring out the best in us, where temptation to sin seeks to bring out the worst.

> "Start by doing what is necessary, then do what is possible, and suddenly you are doing the impossible."
>
> –St. Francis of Assisi (1182–1226)

No one faces life without facing temptation. No one is beyond temptation. Charles Stanley listed six things we can do to avoid or handle temptation:[48]

Ask yourself. If I should yield to this temptation, what will be the immediate and future consequence to me and those around me? Am I prepared to pay the price? Is there a better way to get this need met?

Identify your areas of weakness. Be prepared to overcome personal patterns of weakness.

Visualize victory (refuse to be intimidated). Faith is the ability to envision something positive before it ever happens.

Be accountable to a friend (a sponsor or a mentor).

Set aside a daily time of prayer and meditation.

Learn to rely on the Holy Spirit (instead of yourself, your emotions).

Martin Luther once said, "You cannot keep the birds from flying over your head, but you can keep them from building a nest in your hair."[49] Temptation will pester you, but temptation does not have to master you.

Reflective Questions

What is your plan to overcome temptation now? For example, refusing to be intimidated, recognizing patterns of temptation, and acting accordingly, etc.

Request God's help (part of the plan). Every temptation is an opportunity to do what is right—to run to the God who has been running to you.

Day Four: Coming Out from Behind the Mask

~

God has helped us to take off our masks.

Now we come out from behind the curtain and present our real self to others (and ourselves). People will always reject us, discourage us, not accept us, and give us a reason to want to put the mask back on. However, God will continue to show us in His loving way that our mask is simply not necessary anymore.

God-Confidence

Our true self-worth comes from God healing and changing our hearts. He will give you God-confidence, which is different than self-confidence. When we have self-confidence, we believe we have the power to do almost anything. We go it alone. When we gain God-confidence, we believe we can do anything that God gives us to do. There's a big difference.

Most people won't learn about God-confidence because they won't turn to God and seek His advice and counsel. When you have God in your life, you have what it takes to make it happen, to make those critical life changes. Man can't fix a lot of our problems, but if we choose to put our confidence in God, we know the solution will be the right solution.

God loved you enough to make you exactly the way *He* wanted you to be—*in His image*. This knowledge alone should give you God-confidence. I began to observe that more people noticed me when I acquired God-confidence. Nothing on the outside of me was different, but I appeared to exude a radiant glow from the inside that came from spending time with Jesus. Peter spoke about biblical women that made themselves beautiful by reflecting their inner self, which meant living a pure and respectful existence.

When a woman follows God's direction, she receives a special inner beauty that is reflected in her outward appearance. People may not know *why* she's beautiful. In fact, some may say, "She's not what we call a beauty (by our cultural standards), but there is something about her . . . some sort of spiritual beauty." Wouldn't that give you God-confidence?

> "Self-confidence looks inward—God-confidence looks upward."
>
> –Donna Partow[50]

Accepting Yourself

You have made great progress as you have moved through this study. Your journey toward wholeness has begun, and now you can start to *really* live again. Do you feel that you can really accept yourself the way you are? If you said anything but, "Yes, I can," then pray and ask the Lord to show you how you can begin to accept yourself.

Dr. Gregory Jantz said,

When you can accept yourself, you can laugh again—at yourself and others. Your happiness will no longer be based upon the opinions and desires of other people. Fear of rejection by others will no longer hold you prisoner, because you no longer reject yourself and your past. You are learning to really *like* who you are. Perfectionism has shadowed your life. Now reality can help you see yourself clearly. You have learned that it's okay and *perfectly* normal to make mistakes.[51]

This now means *not* watching extreme makeover programming or *Entertainment Tonight* anymore. It means throwing out your Jackie Collins novels and canceling your subscription to *Cosmopolitan*. We want to focus daily on Jesus and not the comparison game that the world plays. You can either live in fear of the dreaded "pooch," or live your life for God. *Perfection never lasts—but character is forever.*

Reflection

Write out and finish this sentence: "I have God-confidence today because . . ."

Thank God for making you the way He did. That includes those features and areas of your body that you don't like, the ones that make you the "unique you."

Day Five: Restoring God's Temple

~

Your body is the temple of the Holy Spirit.

From the day you began this study, you have been given tools to restore God's temple, your body. Remember the lame man in John 5? Before Jesus healed him, Jesus asked, "Do you want to be healed?" You are the only one who can make a commitment to reach out and use your God-tools.

We Are God's

Before we accepted Jesus Christ, we were all slaves to sin. When we decided to follow Jesus, we stepped out in faith, made Jesus our Lord, and became God's. Belonging to God means true freedom and righteousness.

The Bible shows us the effect of being a slave to sin had on our lives *in the past*.

Romans 6:19–23:

[19] *I put this in human terms because you are weak in your natural selves. Just as you used to offer the parts of your body in slavery to impurity and to ever-increasing wickedness, so now offer them in slavery to righteousness leading to holiness.* [20] *When you were slaves to sin, you were free from the control of righteousness.* [21] *What benefit did you reap at that time from the things you are now ashamed of? Those things result in death!* [22] *But now that you have been set free from sin and have become slaves to God, the benefit you reap leads*

to holiness, and the result is eternal life. [23] *For the wages of sin is death, but the gift of God is eternal life in Christ Jesus our Lord.*

What is the benefit of being God's now, in the present?

"You have been set free from sin and have become slaves to righteousness" (Romans 6:18).

It's a Fight for Freedom

We all have three enemies that prevent us from walking in faith and forgiveness—Satan, our flesh, and the world we live in. God wants us to walk in His forgiveness and accept it as a free gift; there is no need to continue to feel guilt, shame, or fear.

How Can We Experience Victory?

Victory is possible when we begin to change the way we think and realize that we are both beautiful on the inside as well as the outside. How can we experience victory . . .

• *Over the flesh?* 2 Corinthians 10:5: "We demolish arguments and every pretension that sets itself up against the knowledge of God, and we take captive every thought to make it obedient to Christ" (Week Four).

• *Over Satan?* By putting on the full armor of God (Week Five, Ephesians 6:10–18).

• *Over the world?* 1 John 2:15–17: Do not love the world or anything in the world. If anyone loves the world, the love of the Father is not in him. For everything in the world—the cravings of sinful man, the lust of his eyes and the boasting of what he has and does—comes not from the Father but from the world. The world and its desires pass away, but the man who does the will of God lives forever.

> "It is the glow within that creates beauty. People are like stained glass windows. They sparkle like crystal in the sun. At night they continue to sparkle only if there is light within."
>
> —Unknown

Reflective Questions

In what ways are you still punishing yourself for your behavior(s)?

In the future, when I am confronted with painful circumstances, feelings, and situations, I will:

- Accept . . .
- Forgive (name) for . . .
- Forgive myself for . . .
- Accept God's forgiveness for . . .
- Have hope that . . .
- Have joy in . . .
- Be grateful for . . .
- Look at how I have grown (giving a recent example) . . .
- Help others to grow by . . .

Finale: Week Ten

~

There is joy in the morning.

Whether we realize it or not, *today* we have many things to be joyful for:

• If you woke up this morning with more health than illness, you are more blessed than the million people who won't survive the week.

• If you have never experienced the danger of battle, the loneliness of imprisonment, the agony of torture, or the pangs of starvation, you are ahead of twenty million people around the world.

• If you attend church without fear of harassment, arrest, torture, or death, you are more blessed than almost three billion people in the world.

• If you have food in your refrigerator, clothes on your back, a roof over your head, and a place to sleep, you are richer than seventy-five percent of this world.

• If you have money in the bank and in your wallet, you are among the top eight percent of the worlds wealthy.

• If your parents are still married, you are very rare, especially in the USA.

• If you hold up your head with a smile on your face and are truly thankful, you are blessed because the majority can, but most do not.

• If you can hold someone's hand, hug them, or touch them on the shoulder, you are blessed because you can offer God's healing touch.

• If you can read this, you are more blessed than over two billion people in the world that cannot read anything at all.

• What did you learn from this week's study that you can apply to your life this week?

> Promise to Claim: "So if the Son sets you free, you will be free indeed" (John 8:36).

I Want More Bible Food!
Week Ten: Healing For Life

~

Genesis 25:29–33

☑ Describe a recent time or situation where "life just wasn't fair."

Life isn't fair. But in the midst of our trials and temptations, we can be sure that God's grace is sufficient to allow us to handle anything that comes our way.

Read Genesis 25:29–33

This is a classic story of two brothers. One brother, Esau, the eldest, was given a great birthright (special privileges and advantages belonging to the first-born son among the Jews) and the other brother, Jacob, was to serve him. But Jacob managed to take away Esau's birthright with a little more than the smell of good cooking. To Esau, life was unfair. He was the good son, yet, he lost his birthright—his blessing.

The author of Hebrews uses Esau as an example of one who failed to accept God's grace. In a moment of extreme hunger, Esau despised his birthright in order to gain the temporary satisfaction of his flesh. God's grace was sufficient to help Esau handle his cravings, but Esau didn't accept it (Hebrews 12:16).

What parallel do you see in your life? Journal your answer.

In Genesis 35, Jacob builds an altar to commemorate a special time in his life. He had been running from his angry brother Esau and was afraid. In the dark of the night, God revealed himself to Jacob.

Read Genesis 35:9–14

In the midst of Jacob's fear, God became more real to Jacob than ever before. It is often in those dark, painful, and lonely times that God brings us closer to Him.

Describe a recent moment (in your journal) that God brought you close to Him. Learn to recapture that moment the next time you feel like you're in the cave.

God is the one who gives us the desires of our heart, *not man*. Have you given thought that the reason you hurt so badly is because you sought from man what only God could give you? Flesh fails. *God won't ever fail.*

Week Eleven: Nutrition for Your Temple

~

God invites us to be transformed and changed.

Emotional eating involves two sets of issues and behaviors: (1) those involving relationships with others and ourselves, and (2) those relating to food and nutrition. The first ten weeks focused on the first issue. If you have not read and applied the work of the previous weeks, it would not be wise to continue. The principles probably won't work until you can say that you've changed and that you now love yourself.

Many of us could write books about nutrition and diets. I was obsessed with food, so I majored in nutrition in college . . . while battling bulimia. I would devise my own nutrition plan, but if I got hungry and ate something that wasn't in that plan, then my mind said, "I blew it. I might as well blow it all the way. I'll eat and eat, then purge and exercise." As usual, I lost control.

Restoration isn't about developing a new weight-loss program or coming up with a new way to control our eating—*been there, done that*. We need to add sanity—God—to our behaviors and develop a sensible food plan. With God's help, we can assume greater control as we begin the journey toward new and better eating habits.

After sixteen years of bulimia, I didn't know what it was like to eat like a normal person because I ate in my "secret food boat." Don't all of us hide in a "secret food boat?" We eat and binge there. We hide and hoard food in it. We return to the boat when everyone's gone to bed. We no longer know what it is like to eat food when we're hungry or for the nutritional value.

Proverbs 9:17–18: "Stolen water is sweet; food eaten in secret is delicious! But little do they know that the dead are there, that her guests are in the depths of the grave."

God knows what we do in the "secret food boat" and hates that it is destroying us. He has the answers. He can help us to relearn the art of eating three regular meals again—meals that provide us the much needed strength and stamina we lost a long time ago. Jesus said (the Lord's Prayer):

"Give us today our daily bread" (Matthew 6:11).

"Keep us alive with three square meals" (Matthew 6:11, Msg).

"Give us our food again today, as usual" (Matthew 6:11, TLB).

We are going to look at what God says about food and nutrition. Once we've learned (and believe) that God loves us no matter what we look like, and He thinks we are just *maaav-el-ous,* then normal eating habits will come much easier.

Day One: The Temple of the Holy Spirit

~

Our health needs to be an ongoing priority.

Trusted nutrition expert Dr. Gregory Jantz said, "When your physical body is supported, it can help you find the self-confidence and encouragement to deal with the important emotional, relational, and spiritual issues that need to be addressed in your long-term recovery."[52]

There is a story of Reverend Jones, who was working in his garden when along came a parishioner. "My, Reverend, doesn't God make a nice garden?" The reverend replied, "Yes, but you should have seen it before I got here."[53] The point is that God does His part, and we are expected to do our part. The reverend and God partnered to bring about exuberant health and long life. "For we are God's fellow workers; you are God's field, God's building" (1 Corinthians 3:9).

I suggest you locate and work with a professional nutritionist and/or a preventative-minded physician who understands nutrition. That person can develop a personal program around your specific needs. God put every one of us on this earth to fulfill an assignment. How can we fill our assignments if we're weak, undernourished, overweight, and not healthy? We need to be healthy in order to be strong. The Lord is our strength!

The Old Testament (Genesis 5) tells us that many of God's people lived to a ripe, old age—some nine hundred years! Older women were fertile, and older men were virile (Genesis 21:1–8). Dr. Patrick Quillan said,

Scientists have been accumulating data, which proves the merits of the biblical diet and lifestyle. We were created by God with certain physical requirements. If we do not meet these needs, then the body does not function well. After years of struggling to perform in spite of poor conditions, the body eventually gives out in disease and early death. *But don't blame God. God gave us free will to make our own choices in life.*[54]

1 Corinthians 8:9 warns us: "Be careful, however, that the exercise of your freedom does not become a stumbling block to the weak." Over time, we have misused our freedom and have chosen the wrong foods and lifestyle.

The Bible also tells us, "Do you not know that your body is a temple of the Holy Spirit, who is in you, whom you have received from God? You are not your own; you were bought at a price. Therefore honor God with your body" (1 Corinthians 6:19–20).

> "The mind is the driver of change but your body is the vehicle that gets you there."
>
> –Dr. Gregory Jantz

Reflective Questions

Would you agree that much of your suffering, illness, and tears are because you are not doing your part?

Do you think your health problems may be self-inflicted because you are not following God's plan (His Word)?

Day Two: God's Covenant

Is food a blessing or just filling the void?

Did you know that in Abraham's era, food was a visible means of knowing that there was a God? Plants provided food, medicine, clothing, dyes for painting and writing. The animals provided food. Thanksgiving was offered at each meal because food was an intimate link with God. Food was a sign of God's generosity and a symbol of His miraculous power.

Jesus is represented in the symbol of a fish. He converted water into wine for His first miracle (John 2:9). Jesus used bread and wine in the Passover Feast as symbols of His body and blood to be sacrificed at Calvary (Luke 22:19–21). Food was a covenant between God and His people.

When the Israelites were wandering in the desert, God sent them "manna." Exodus 16:31–32:

The people of Israel called the bread manna. It was white like coriander seed and tasted like wafers made with honey. Moses said, "This is what the Lord has commanded: 'Take an omer of manna and keep it for the generations to come, so they can see the bread I gave you to eat in the desert when I brought you out of Egypt.'"

Manna was new to their diet and gave them much nourishment. God also used the manna as an instrument to teach the Israelites an important lesson, a lesson we can also learn from.

"Each morning everyone gathered as much as he needed, and when the sun grew hot, it melted away" (Exodus 16:21). The key is "daily." The Israelites asked for what they needed on a daily basis. God wants to be with us on a daily basis. He wants us to ask Him for the desires and needs of our heart every day. Don't wait for the outward need before you seek Him with your obvious daily need.

Ponder this verse: "He humbled you, causing you to hunger and then feeding you with manna, which neither you nor your fathers had known, to teach you that man does not live on bread alone but on *every word* that comes from the mouth of the Lord" (Deuteronomy 8:3).

Today, we look at food either as a blessing or as something to fill the void in our soul. When we eat, or control what we don't eat, we receive immediate gratification and pleasure. However, that feeling doesn't make the problem(s) go away.

Some think that God will love us more if we eat the food He's blessed us with, so we overeat (gluttony). When we eat this way, we have ignored God's purpose for providing food—to nourish our body with essential nutrients and to provide a connection with God.

> "The biggest seller is cookbooks and the second is diet books—how not to eat what you've just learned to cook."
> –Andy Rooney[55]

There is an age-old saying that God feeds the birds, but He doesn't throw the food into their nests. The birds have to get their own food. We have the potential of living a vibrantly healthy life. However, we have to earn it through new lifestyle practices.

Reflective Question

The more you cry out to God and ask for wisdom and strength, the more He will give you the insight you need. What wisdom do you need from God today regarding your eating habits and meal plan?

Day Three: Putting Words into Action

~

Time to devise an action plan.

Most likely, you know how you should eat, but you probably find it too difficult to put that knowledge into practice. Dr. Gregory Jantz says,

I never ask anyone to go on a diet. Both the initial and ultimate false premise of a diet is that *food is the culprit*. Food is not the problem, and, therefore, food is not the cure. The antidote to dieting—is to live a truly authentic, balanced, healthy life as a person who is growing into the individual God created you to be.[56]

If you are like me, you will most likely *hate* your new food plan—initially. We hate change and discipline, don't we? Again, we are asked to submit ourselves to doing something God's way. 1 Corinthians 9:27 reads, "Like an athlete I punish my body, treating it roughly, training it to do what it should, not what it wants to." We are actually making our body our slave, instead of us being a slave to our body (TLB).

"Speak It Out"

I hope "Speak It Out" has become part of your daily routine. You can apply the same principle as you make the change to a healthy food plan. When you begin to feel tempted or weak, pull out one of your favorite memory verses. Tape the verse (or a prayer) to your refrigerator or your computer at work, the places where you are most vulnerable. We need God to help us everyday in this area of our life too. If you don't have any favorite verses, select a few of these and personalize them:

1. "He gives strength to the weary and increases the power of the weak" (Isaiah 40:29). *God gives me strength and power when I'm weak.*

2. "Commit to the Lord whatever you do, and your plans will succeed" (Proverbs 16:3). *I commit my food plan to you, Father, and I will succeed!*

3. "I can do everything through him who gives me strength" (Philippians 4:13). *I have God's strength. I can follow this plan!*

4. "The Lord will fight for you; you need only to be still" (Exodus 14:14). *The Lord is fighting for me, I just need to relax and rest in Him.*

5. "This is my work, and I can do it only because Christ's mighty energy is at work within me" (Colossians 1:29, TLB).

6. "The Lord is a strong fortress. The godly run to him and are safe" (Proverbs 18:10, TLB). *The Lord is my fortification. He will get me through my food plan today.*

Paul wrote, "No discipline seems pleasant at the time, but painful. Later on, however, it produces a harvest of righteousness and peace for those who have been trained by it" (Hebrews 12:11).

Change is tough, but try to view it as medicine. At first, it's unpleasant to take, but it eventually restores strength and wholeness.

> "Since Eve ate the apple, much depends on dinner."
> –Lord Byron

Reflective Question

What are three foods that make you feel energetic and alive? Why or how so?

Day Three: Proper Eating and Exercise

~

What do thin, healthy people eat?

I studied those people as well as the people in the Bible. They ate what they wanted. I realized that all along, my mother was a good example. I've never seen her deprive herself of "bad" foods. So I started to follow her example:

Do not avoid everything "bad," but eat in moderation. If you want a slice of pizza, have a slice. Have two, depending on how wide they are cut. Not three or four slices. Include a dark green salad. It's moderation—not deprivation!

Eat until you are full. Many of us feel obligated to eat everything on our plates. If you're at a restaurant and they serve you a man-size meal (which most do today), don't feel like you have to eat it all. Take half home and eat it later when you're hungry.

Do not diet or skip meals in order to lose weight. Statistically, diets usually equal failure, and they emphasize what is wrong instead of what is right. They encourage competition and comparison. Totie Fields (American actress popular in the 50's) said, "I've been on a diet for two weeks, and all I've lost is fourteen days."

Eating in Moderation

God wants balance in your life, and one area is eating in moderation. The concept is scriptural.

• Proverbs 23:1–3: "When you sit to dine with a ruler, note well what is before you, and put a knife to your throat if you are given to gluttony. Do not crave his delicacies, for that food is deceptive."

• Proverbs 25:16: "If you find honey, eat just enough—too much of it, and you will vomit."

In Daniel 1, King Nebuchadnezzar took the Israelites hostage. The king was generous and provided well for the hostages, offering them a royal feast. Verse 5 says, "The king assigned them a daily amount of food and wine from the king's table." When the king offered such delicacies to Daniel (1:8), "Daniel resolved not to defile himself with the royal food and wine, and he asked the chief official for permission not to defile himself this way."

What does the verse mean, "Not to defile himself?"

Daniel made a personal decision about what he would eat. Unlike many of us, he did not let food define who he was. He decided what was good for him, his total body, and soul. Since the king's delicacies had been offered to idols, Daniel knew that those delicacies were not good for him (body and soul). He successfully resisted the lure of the world and experienced the rewards of God's favor.

Daniel triumphed over his appetite. Scripture reveals the secret that Daniel used to conquer the world. He made a vow ahead of time to prepare for worldly temptations: "Daniel made up his mind not to eat the food" (1:8, TLB).

Your Metabolism

Your metabolism (how much energy you burn) goes up and down depending on how much you eat. If you are trying to lose weight, and you only eat one meal a day with a snack, you may be lowering your metabolism. This makes it harder for your body to lose weight.

Think of your metabolism like a fire. In order to get the fire going, you must start with small pieces (kindling) so the fire can build. As it gets hotter and stronger, you add big pieces (logs). But you wouldn't start the fire with a log, would you? The best way to raise your metabolism so that you can eat more food without gaining weight is by eating smaller, more frequent meals. This is how my mother eats.

☑ Write out and finish this sentence in your journal: "If I honor and respect my body (temple) daily, it will . . ."

Exercise

Some of you are compulsive over-exercisers, and others think a dumbbell is an idiot. I was the first. As a jogger, my knees took an intense pounding day after day after day. I had two arthroscopic surgeries on both knees. God didn't design our bodies to run daily marathons (even though everyone at the gym praises the accomplishment).

As my thinking began to change, my rigid regimen began to relax. I could see how compulsive my routine was. It's important to exercise, but it's also important to listen to your body and not take it to extremes. Believe me—you will pay for it later.

For those of you that hate exercise, it may be because you see exercise as a set of rules that can't be broken (like the word *diet*). Yes, there are rules for holy living and your household (Colossians 3), but throw out any preconceived rules about exercise. You don't have to join a gym. Begin by simply walking. *No one is going to judge you.*

> "We first make our habits, and then our habits make us."
> –John Dryden (1631–1700)

Reflective Question

How can you apply Daniel's experience to your life?

Day Four: Basic Steps to a Healthy Diet

~

Talk with a professional before starting any new eating plan.

Enlist the help of a family member or friend to give you support and help you stay on track. The challenge is to create an eating plan that you can live with and includes healthy foods.

"When dining with a rich man, be on your guard and don't stuff yourself, though it all tastes so good" (Proverbs 23:1, TLB).

Steps to good nutrition come from a diet that: [57]

• Is balanced with foods from all groups that include several servings of fruits and vegetables (a variety of each, five to nine servings each day), and grains (especially whole grains, a good source of fiber).

• Is low in saturated fat and cholesterol, and moderate in total fat intake. Less than ten percent of your daily calories should come from saturated fat, and less than thirty percent of your daily calories should come from total fat.

• Has a limited number of calories from sugars (candy, cookies, and cakes).

• Has foods prepared with less sodium or salt—no more than 2,400 milligrams of sodium per day, or about one teaspoon of salt per day for a healthy heart.

Fasting

As Christians, fasting can be an excellent spiritual discipline. I would caution you against fasting until you have completely healed from any disordered eating.

What if I Binge?

When I started following a healthy food plan, there were days when I wanted a second serving or to eat desert. In my mind I knew it was okay once in awhile, but Satan would bait me. He knew I promised myself that I wouldn't purge, so he cunningly told me I should take laxatives instead to get rid of the fat (although I know now that laxatives don't do that). This is *not* an option!

I found that my body could digest more food than I thought. I was so used to thinking that if I went one ounce over my food plan, I'd gain a couple pounds. Guess what? I didn't! If I go out to lunch and eat more than I'm comfortable with, I listen to my stomach. Usually, I only want a small dinner. My body compensates for the change, and I don't gain extra weight.

How I Avoid Binging

• I ask myself what my motive is for eating. Am I really hungry, or is it because I'm bored, stressed, fearful, or depressed? If so, I leave the so-called binge environment. I also ask, "Have I had enough sleep and exercise?" These are often the reasons I binge.

• Drink a liter of water and wait fifteen minutes. I might have a couple of soda crackers (they expand in your stomach). Delaying eating is good discipline. It helps me to stop and think about my goals, and often the craving will pass.

• Begin an enjoyable task immediately after eating a meal, such as crafts, classes, and hobbies.

• Pack healthy and satisfying food to take to work instead of buying out.

• I have a support network of a few friends to call when I'm feeling vulnerable.

• Pray and repeat Scripture: "How sweet are *your words* to my taste, sweeter than honey to my mouth!" (Psalms 119:103)

It's progress, not perfection. It's okay to be imperfect.

Identifying Triggers

A trigger is a signal, a temptation, which precedes a binge or compulsive overeating episode. It is important to identify triggers and avoid them. Most often, triggers are situations and/or emotions you are often not even aware of.

For example, I know my triggers and will journal when temptation calls. I will document binge episodes. What happened right before I binged? For example, did I see a TV commercial for McDonalds, or did I have an argument with my husband?

Discuss with another person a plan for eating out, dining alone, stressful situations, and other scenarios the group deems important.

Reflective Question

Can you be the person God created you to be by following a healthy, supervised food plan? Why or why not?

Finale: Week Eleven

Jesus said, "No servant can serve two masters. Either he will hate the one and love the other, or he will be devoted to the one and despise the other" (Luke 16:13). It is about making a choice. A successful program and lifestyle is about making the right choices. As we let go of the lies we have believed, forgive ourselves and others, and make restitution, we come to terms with the fact we can eat properly again.

God created so many delicious and exotic foods for our pleasure and nourishment. But we must remember that He created them as fuel for our bodies so that we can function properly. Thank God for your body. He gave each and every one of us an incredible body. We need to begin to praise Him regularly for it.

Who is made in the image of God? Speak it out: *I am made in the image of God!* Learning to eat healthy is not an end in itself; it's the beginning of more important transformations to come. Make a commitment to take care of yourself. Your body is God's gift to you; please treat it as one!

What did you learn from this week's study that you can apply to your life this week?

> Promise to Claim: "Jesus declared, 'I am the bread of life. He who comes to me will never go hungry, and he who believes in me will never be thirsty'" (John 6:35).

I Want More Bible Food!
Week Eleven: Nutrition for Your Temple

~

Mark 1

☑ Where does meal preparation and eating fall in your daily priorities? Is it #1, #2, #3? Make a list and explain.

Are you familiar with John the Baptist? If so, you probably groaned when you read that he lived on a steady diet of grasshoppers. True. Read Mark 1:6.

He probably ate a steady diet of them because they were convenient, the fast food of that century. What I like about John is that food is not very important to him. He had far more important things to take care of.

We can learn from John the Baptist. John ate to live. He did not live to eat.

Can you say the same? Why or why not?

_____

_____

_____

John was busy serving his master, Jesus. Who are you busy serving?

Food was his servant, not his best friend or replacement for life.

_____

_____

_____

Reflect on these words. How can you apply them to your particular situation?

_____

_____

_____

Read 1 Corinthians 10:25–33. How does someone eat to the glory of God?

_____

_____

_____

_____

_____

_____

How can doing everything to the glory of God change not only what you do, but how you do it? Give some examples.

_____

_____

_____

_____

_____

_____

Week Twelve: The Road to Damascus

~

I'm glowing from the inside out!

Before starting this study, we spent too much time focusing on our outside. We've begun now to see and feel our beauty radiate from the inside. We're headed toward *total* vibrancy and health.

Our faith and healing are not complete until we take what we've learned and experienced and give it to others in need. When God created us in His image, He intended that we pour ourselves into one another. That's part of total health.

Do you know a woman or teenager who *never* makes a negative comment about herself? I doubt it, because it is a cultural epidemic. Our mission is to tell others the message about God and His healing power and show them by example how it works.

I've learned that God allows us to go through our life collecting experiences, like bargains at a sale. Then the day comes when we look into our basket of goodies, and we see a whole array of stories and experiences that God has weaved together to be used in our special ministry—a ministry custom designed for each and every one of us. You may not be called to teach or speak on the subject, but there are abundant opportunities for you to take your message—your story.

If you are a mother or a role model (teacher, coach or mentor), your realm of influence is great. Remember the saying *Like mother, like daughter*. How often does your daughter and/or son hear you talk about dieting, your appearance, or what others say or think about you? (Eating disorders are on the rise in young boys).

Dr. Larry Crabb said,

The act of giving itself provides the nourishment our soul's desire . . . In the middle of our difficult lives, the gospel of Jesus Christ builds a bridge between us and God and between us and other people. As we learn to walk across that bridge to connect with God and with his people, we will come alive. Struggles will continue, but they will be nudged out of the center of our lives by the reality of meaning, joy, perseverance, and love. *Life in Christ, together: that's our hope.*[58]

Remember, *God does not ask your ability or your inability. He asks only your availability.*

Day One: Your Road to Damascus
[Steps Ten & Eleven]

~

The hardest part of the healing journey is that it requires us to change.

We've been seeking help for a long time. We've been inspired by other people's restoration and testimonies, but the actual doing is hard because we have to change, and change is difficult. However, change is the most wonderful part of the healing process. God has given us the ability to change and grow. He works within us to strengthen us, heal us, and make us new. Saul's conversion is an example of such change.

We read in Acts 9:1–22 about Saul (better known as Paul). He grew up trying to follow perfectionism and unattainable standards set by the religious fundamentalists of his day. He thought his salvation was dependant on obeying those standards. His strict adherence to the law of Moses and the traditions of the Pharisees led him into struggles and conflicts with early Christians. Saul threw Christians out of synagogues and had them executed. It took a dramatic act of God to redirect Saul's passion.

While he was on the road to arrest the Christians in Damascus, Jesus confronted Saul. Saul lost his sight and regained it three days later. He then saw the truth. His conversion from religious perfectionism to the grace that is in Christ Jesus is the road of healing for all of us that discover the inadequacy of anything that is performance-based.

God is trying to get our attention, calling us out of the pit of abnormal eating. Do you see that healing is not something you can attain, but something offered to you—a special gift?

Like Saul, we've been blind for years, perhaps decades. Now our sight is restored and we are ready for the next step—God's special plan for our life.

He invites us to embrace salvation and a new life. "'For I know the plans I have for you,' declares the Lord, 'plans to prosper you and not to harm you, plans to give you hope and a future'" (Jeremiah 29:11).

You can't know God's plan unless you know Him. *Today is your road to Damascus experience.* God is calling you out.

> "Ask and seek, and your heart will grow big enough to receive him and to keep him as your own. Wherever God has put you, that is your vocation. It is not what we do but how much love we put into it."
>
> —Mother Teresa[59]

Reflective Questions

Has God spoken to you about reaching out to help others?

How do you feel about reaching out? Describe in detail.

Day Two: A New Creation in Jesus Christ

~

Do you know who you are and where you stand?

It's important before you hit the road to Damascus that you know that. Would you say that you are a new creation in Jesus Christ? *Yes.* The following verses describe who you are in Christ.

What does each verse mean to you personally?

• 2 Corinthians 3:17–18: "Now the Lord is the Spirit, and where the Spirit of the Lord is, there is freedom. And we, who with unveiled faces all reflect the Lord's glory, are being transformed into his likeness with ever-increasing glory, which comes from the Lord, who is the Spirit."

• 1 Peter 2:9: "But you are a chosen people, a royal priesthood, a holy nation, a people belonging to God, that you may declare the praises of him who called you out of darkness into his wonderful light."

• 2 Corinthians 5:17: "Therefore, if anyone is in Christ, he is a new creation; the old has gone, the new has come!"

We each have a unique position in God's family. Again, what does each verse personally mean to you?

• Ephesians 1:4–5: "He predestined us to be adopted as his sons (daughters) through Jesus Christ, in accordance with his pleasure and will."

• Romans 8:17: "Now if we are children, then we are heirs—heirs of God and co-heirs with Christ, if indeed we share in his sufferings in order that we may also share in his glory."

Long before any one of us was born, God decided to adopt us into His family through His son, Jesus Christ. If Jesus is the King, what does that make you?

Yes, a princess! Not the princess you dressed up as when you were a wee-one, but true royalty—and heir to the King. How does that make you feel now?

> "When I take another's needs into consideration and bend, I spiritually stretch."
>
> –Helene Lerner-Robbins

No One is Righteous. As the Scriptures say:

> [10] *No one is good—no one in all the world is innocent.* [11] *No one has ever really followed God's paths or even truly wanted to.* [12] *Every one has turned away; all have gone wrong. No one anywhere has kept on doing what is right; not one.* [13] *Their talk is foul and filthy like the stench from an open grave. Their tongues are loaded with lies. Everything they say has in it the sting and poison of deadly snakes.* [14] *Their mouths are full of cursing and bitterness.* [15] *They are quick to kill, hating anyone who disagrees with them.* [16] *Wherever they go they leave misery and trouble behind them,* [17] *and they have never known what it is to feel secure or enjoy God's blessing.* [18] *They care nothing about God nor what he thinks of them.* Romans 3:10–18 (TLB):

☑ Before you started this study, would you say this passage described you? Today, rewrite this passage in your journal using what God has taught you. You may want to write it using your present feelings or projecting into the near future (your desired change).

Reflective Question

What is different about being in God's family, versus your own family?

Day Three: Serving God

I am created for God. He made me.

Oswald Chambers wrote,

> The whole human race was created to glorify God and enjoy Him forever. Sin has switched the human race on to another track, but it has not altered God's purpose in the tiniest degree; and when we are born again, we are brought into the realization of God's great purpose for the human race. We have to maintain our soul open to the fact of God's creative purpose, and not muddle it with our own intentions. If we do, God will have to crush our intentions on one side however much it may hurt. The purpose for which the missionary is created is that he may be God's servant, one in whom God is glorified. When once we realize that through the salvation of Jesus Christ we are made perfectly fit for God, we shall understand why Jesus Christ is so ruthless in His demands. *He demands absolute rectitude (righteousness) from His servants, because He has put into them the very nature of God.*[60]

Once we are born again, God has certain expectations. Scripture says "you are a guide for the blind, and a light for those who are in the dark" (Romans 2:19).

> "The only ones of you who will be truly happy are those who have found and learned how to serve."
>
> —Albert Schweitzer

.

Christ's Representatives

In the classic movie *It's a Wonderful Life,* George Bailey discovered this truth. Though he had many opportunities to pursue his ambitions elsewhere, George remained in his community and was dedicated to providing affordable housing to its members. When his guardian angel showed him what the town would be like if he had never been born, Bailey realized how much of a difference his giving had made. George also discovered another secret—*that what you give is what you receive.* Whatever you give out comes back to you.

When you extend yourself to nurture the spiritual growth of another, you nurture your own growth. Although his material possessions were modest, George Bailey was toasted the *richest* man in town by the people of Bedford Falls. Later he remarked, "No man can be poor as long as he has friends." Bailey gave of himself for the joy of giving, and joy is what he received. By following this path, we, too, can be blessed.

> "Do not follow where the path may lead. Go instead where there is no path and leave a trail."
>
> –George Bernard Shaw (1856–1950)

Staying Rooted

It's so easy to get caught up in the things that the world has to offer. Sometimes our faith takes a backseat and we don't even realize it. The only way to determine who God truly wants us to be is to stay rooted in His Word daily. God intends to use us to persuade men and women to drop their differences and enter into God's work.

Psalm 1:1–3 says,

[1] *Blessed is the man who does not walk in the counsel of the wicked or stand in the way of sinners or sit in the seat of mockers.* [2] *But his delight is in*

the law of the Lord, and on his law he meditates day and night. ³ *He is like a tree planted by streams of water, which yields its fruit in season and whose leaf does not wither. Whatever he does prospers.*

Just think how much more surely the blood of Christ will transform our lives and hearts. "His sacrifice frees us from the worry of having to obey the old rules and makes us want to serve the living God" (Hebrews 9:14, TLB).

Isn't it comforting to know that we are each God's workmanship, created in Christ Jesus to do good works, which God prepared in advance for us to do (Ephesians 2:10).

Are you ready to find out what your destiny is?

☑ Brainstorm about helping others with abnormal eating patterns, even if you are not doing this in a group setting. Throw every idea on the table—no matter how trivial you may think it is. Get others to help you.

Day Four: God's Plan

~

We were so certain we knew what was best.

We thought our motives would guarantee happiness. As we reflect, we see our wishes didn't come true. Did any one of us expect to be to be reading this book or participating in a support group? That wasn't my plan!

We probably expected to have children by a certain age, a particular kind of spouse, a certain career. Did we really anticipate this? Addiction, obsessiveness, and then freedom from it were not part of the deal. *But it does fit into the big plan!* The happiness we experience today as we learn and grow in Jesus doesn't compare to what we anticipated a few years back.

I swam in victory after God healed and delivered me from bulimia and substance abuse. No longer the victim, He gave me something no person could—freedom. I became *a victor—a survivor.*

I knew whatever other problems I would face He would be there to get me through. I sought the Lord with all my heart. I asked Him what He had in mind for my life. Instead of telling the Lord where I wanted to be, I asked the Lord to place me where I would fit in, where I was needed. I found *complete peace* after I found the Lord's plan for my life (and He didn't send me out to a mission field in Africa!).

> "Success has nothing to do with what you gain in life or accomplish for yourself. Success is what you do for others."
>
> –Danny Thomas (1914–1991)

Giving Back God's Love

God is love. That is why we are here, to be loved by God. Everything God has done, He did with us in mind—from creation to redemption. Redemption means we have been bought out of sin and slavery (bondage). We were bought with Jesus Christ's blood, not gold or silver—His blood. When we comprehend that sacrifice, and how much God loves us, we change. We don't live for *self* anymore. We begin to give of ourselves.

> "Example is not the main thing in influencing others. It is the only thing."
>
> –Albert Schweitzer (1875–1965)

Helping Others
[Step 12]

Prepare for Change. If God asks you to do something, He will enable you to do it. God is all-powerful, and He can make it possible for you to do His will. You will know when your life is in the middle of God's action. His ways and thoughts are so different from ours. They often sound either wrong or completely crazy. We need the readiness to believe Him and trust Him completely. We need to believe that what He is doing is the best for us. We should never second-guess Him—just let God be God.

Find a Healthy Church Community. We all want a church where we feel welcomed, a place to belong. It also important to find a church that nurtures your gifts and allows you to produce fruit and help others (see Appendix D: Finding a Healthy Church Community).

Use Your Testimony. When I first decided to "come out" and share my story, I went overboard. I was full of vigor and sparkle. However, my attitude came across as cockiness. Some would say I was arrogant and prideful. Learn from my example. Satan will not be happy with you for tempting to free his captives. He will try repeatedly to get you to fall again, and this is one of his methods. Don't get discouraged! Put your armor on every day. Add prayer and practice. Your testimony will shine! God will use you at the right time in the right place. I believe that God expects us to use our stories (and gifts) that He has given us. Each *test* built your *test*imony.

Ask God to use you for His glory. Look for an opportunity to tell someone about the healing and miracles He has done in your life. If you ask Him to use you to encourage someone else, He will. Your problems will begin to seem less overwhelming. God will begin working them out for you. My greatest rewards have come when I have focused on inspiring others and pointing them to God.

A wise person once said that to the world, you might be only one small person, but to one person, you just might be the world. Pray, "God grant me the serenity to accept the people I cannot change, the courage to change the 'one' I can change, and the wisdom to know that it's me."[61]

You may be thinking that the world is so big and your lamp so small and unimportant. Nothing could be further from the truth. We can all light something each day. It all begins with the desire expressed in Michelangelo's prayer: "God grant me the desire always to desire to be more than I can ever accomplish."

When you enter into a relationship with God, He reveals His will and invites you to join Him in the work He is doing. I can tell you, when you see through His Word that God does pursue a love relationship with you and does have a purpose for your life, you will literally be filled with tears of happiness. I found a real joy that comes when God calls, and I can say, "Coming Lord!"

Steps To Writing Your Testimony

1. Depend on the power of God for your outline. Pray for clear and loving communication.
2. Begin by outlining what strong emotion, attitude, or con-

cern you had before you knew Jesus. For example, need for love and acceptance, fear, anger, the obsession to be a size two.

3. Answer the question, "What is my purpose?" and then think of some illustrations. Other questions to ponder are, "What emotions did I experience while living through this?" "What spiritual lesson did I learn from this experience?"

4. Write down any Scripture verse or passage that comes to mind as you meditate on what happened. Give just enough detail to arouse interest, not a blow-by-blow description of every incident.

5. Remember your focus is on the solution—Jesus Christ—not on you and your problems. Every illustration and idea that you present should be tied into the purpose of presenting Jesus Christ.

6. Continue to study the Bible to increase your knowledge and understanding of who God is. Grow in your awareness of what God is doing in your life and how you can impact the lives of others.

Day Five: Our Path

⁓

Are you ready to open a special present?

When I was a youngster, I couldn't wait until my birthday and Christmas to open all those wonderful gifts. Months before, I'd start counting the days off in anticipation of opening that special gift I had been dreaming about. Following God's purposeful path is like celebrating your birthday and Christmas all year long. I imagine that I'm following the "yellow brick road" (in the Wizard of Oz). All along this long, windy, golden path (which leads into unknown territory), God leaves presents.

I never know where the presents will be, or when I'll find one. But when I find that one present, I know it holds an incredible gift—a gift that no one else can give me.

Sometimes, we are given a present that we don't see or want to open. Other times, we begin to open the present and realize it's not for us. Someone once told me that a present was called that because it is *presented* to that person. *It isn't a gift until it is opened and received.* I pray you will find all of your presents along your yellow brick path. "Your word is a lamp to my feet and a light for my path" (Psalms 119:105).

> "Be prepared at all times for the gifts of God and be ready always for new ones. For God is a thousand times more ready to give than we are."
>
> —Meister Eckhart[62]

Choose Your Path

Ralph Marston said,

The footprints you leave behind show clearly where you have been. Yet they do not dictate where you can now go. Perhaps your life up to now has been difficult and filled with disappointment. None of that matters when it comes to the choices now available to you. At this moment in time, you can go in any direction you choose. [63]

We've arrived! Now we can benefit from what we've learned and experienced. After dissecting our past, we have a much better idea of where we truly want to go. Look back at your footprints and decide where the next set will lead.

You have another choice to make right now. Your possibilities are limitless as you take the Lord's hand.

> "Errors and mistakes are the necessary steps in the learning process; once they have served their purpose, they should be forgotten."
>
> –Vince Lombardi (1913–1970)

Helping Others with Disordered Eating

If you know or suspect someone else close to you is struggling with disordered eating, go to God first. It won't help the situation to force them to eat or not eat. Here is a list of do's and don'ts:

Do Not

- Think you're the expert and have the answer.
- Get into a power struggle over food with her or him.
- Blame yourself or your husband/wife (his/her "insensitive" remarks are often made the culprit).

• Make her or him feel guilty, angry, or bad for the choices she or he has made.

Do

• In a loving way, confront the person. Continue to show love throughout the whole process by listening, hugging, etc.

• Encourage her or him to seek a professional (counselor, pastor, support group) and recognize that the problem isn't "food."

• Require her or him to be accountable to herself/himself and someone else.

Parents have a huge impact on their children. The choices you make may be mimicked by your daughter (or son). *This is important:* Do you constantly talk about dieting and your body? Do you eat properly? Does your child hear you purging?

Reflective Questions

Who might be watching your life today, observing your decisions as you choose between loving Jesus and loving the world?

What activities and commitments in your life are keeping you from loving and serving Christ with all your heart? Ask yourself: "Will my involvement in these things make any difference ten years from now . . . or in eternity?"

Finale: Week Twelve

~

Serving my purpose in life is only a small repayment for God's gift of healing.

"You did not choose me, but I chose you and appointed you to go and bear fruit—fruit that will last. Then the Father will give you whatever you ask in my name" (John 15:1). This is a wonderful promise, a promise I received from my Father.

I want to share my devotional prayer with you:

Lord, what motivates me at this moment is being effective for You. I praise You for what You've done in my life. You have become my daily food and nourishment, my best friend, my counselor, my teacher, and my mentor. You are my oxygen. Without Your kind of air, I may have died. If not, I would most certainly be living an unworthy life, most likely in the grips of addiction and self-destruction. You, Lord, not only saved my life physically, but spiritually. You have given life new meaning. My life is simpler today because I focus on You. My life is fulfilled today because I focus on You. Lord, I trust You completely and have faith You will carry me to a higher plane and far better places than I could doing it my way. As our relationship grows everyday, I feel Your love—it's the water of my life. I need You to take care of me. I fear if I turn my back to You, the old Kimberly will reemerge. You are my daily bread. Lord, my prayer to You is the one that never fails, "Thy will be done."

I can tell you firsthand, knowing your purpose will give meaning to your life. One day, we will all stand before God, and He will do an audit of our lives before we can enter eternity with Him (Romans 14:10–12).

My final question to you is, "Does your life point people to the love and goodness of God?"

Promise To Claim: "For we are God's workmanship, created in Christ Jesus to do good works, which God prepared in advance for us to do" (Ephesians 2:10).

I Want More Bible Food!
Week Twelve: The Road to Damascus

Joshua 2

Describe an obstacle you overcame. What was it about the situation that motivated you to run down that obstacle?

Read Joshua 2.

Rahab the prostitute is the woman who made Israel's advance into Jericho possible because she hid Joshua's spies in her home. Rahab was given a choice. She could have sent the spies away and continued to live as a prostitute, or she could make herself available to God and become a woman of faith.

What did Rahab choose to do? What obstacles did she face?

_____

_____

_____

_____

_____

_____

Our God is the God of second chances and the God of restoration. We have a choice to make—to move forward in faith or stay as we are. Rahab was not afraid of risk. She pushed her past aside and didn't allow it to stand in the way of her new beginning.

Read Hebrews 11:31. Are you surprised that Rahab is listed as a member of the "Faith Hall of Fame"? Would you say you have the same kind of faith? Why or why not?

_____

_____

_____

_____

_____

Our lives do count as long as we place them in God's hands. Rahab escaped the destruction that came on those who refused to trust God.

Week Thirteen: Final Instructions

~

Celebrate!

Take the time to celebrate—your growth, your new relationship in Christ, and your success. Celebrate who you are now—a child of God. You're beautiful, a delight, and pure joy. No longer do you have to be better, perfect, or something that you are not. Your beauty shines from your inside, a radiant glow that others don't have.

For each milestone you reach, pause, reflect, and rejoice. Celebrate your new life and everything that is good.

Melody Beattie said, "Celebration is a high form of praise, of gratitude to the Creator for the beauty of God's creation. To enjoy and celebrate the good does not mean that it will be taken from you. To celebrate is to delight in the gift, to show gratitude." [64]

Day One: Speak it Out

~

Remember, *progress*, not perfection!

Maybe you are not where you want to be yet, but thank God that you are not where you used to be.

Here are more daily affirmations to *speak out:*

• I have a purpose. God has given me a road map for living, and I am in charge and in control.

• I have a plan. God has shown me where I am going and given me His Word to live by.

• God is with me every second of every day. I can talk to Him about anything at any time and He will gladly listen.

• I am taking full responsibility for my food choices and life decisions.

• Everyday I am building a strong spiritual foundation. Dr. Gregory Jantz said, "A strong spiritual foundation is characterized by a daily attitude of gratitude, a spirit of courage, the practice of patience, and the joys of self-discipline."

• God made my body His temple—I am learning to love my body, His temple.

I am too blessed to be stressed or depressed and too anointed to be disappointed!

Someone once said that the shortest distance between a problem and a solution is the distance between your knees and the floor. The one who kneels to God can stand up to anything.

> "Always bear in mind that your own resolution to succeed is more important than any other one thing."
>
> –Abraham Lincoln (1809–1865)

Reflective Question

Are there any steps left that you need to take to make God number one in your life? Be willing to seek regular accountability from a Christian friend.

Day Two: The Elements of Freedom

~

What do we have in common?

When I look at all the people who have successfully healed from disordered eating or a negative body image, the common elements are:

- Received Jesus as Lord and Savior.
- Kept focused on Jesus *daily* and said *thank-you.*
- Stayed rooted in His Word and replaced lies with the truth.
- Received forgiveness for their past mistakes and have forgiven those who hurt them.
- Received a new heart and spirit that came with a whole new set of godly desires.
- Developed an awareness of her/his positive features and accepted what she/he could not change.
- Replaced destructive eating habits with a healthy meal plan.
- Had a relapse plan.

These people renewed their minds to God's Word and started to identify with Christ and not their self-centered problems. They found direction and freedom in Jesus. This is a free gift available to anyone.

Relapse Plan

We're human, infallible, and Satan wants us to fall. We've worked so hard at changing our thinking and eating patterns. Most of us will struggle to keep negative body stress, issues of acceptance, and perfection to a minimum. We've talked about it before—be prepared. Here are some more suggestions:

Set realistic expectations. Accept that you will never be perfect and you will have negative thoughts about yourself.

Don't play the comparison game. Focus on yourself, and remember, you don't know what's going on in their "inside." Maybe you're feeling terrific with your new healthy weight and lifestyle. Don't criticize others who don't share your views. Don't accept criticism from others about the way you look or the way you live your life.

Recognize temptation and negative feelings. Know your enemy and know yourself intimately. Anticipate your battles. Put your armor on before going into battle. Fight on your knees (before the temptation comes). You will win the battle.

Avoid stress. Get enough sleep. Don't underestimate the benefit of sleep. You're not "wonder-woman." Sleep is critical to emotional, physical, and spiritual wellness.

Keep an accountability partner and prayer partner. Jesus said, "For where two or three come together in my name, there am I with them" (Matthew 18:20).

Keep Scripture close by. We know the power of the Word, so don't let the enemy sidetrack your efforts. Good, solid Bible teaching is a crucial part of deliverance from the enemy. Join a Bible study group, and reread this study as often as you can. You will find the questions take on a new meaning as you grow and change.

Rebuilding your life is a process—it's a journey that will keep you busy. It's all up to you from this point forward!

Reflective Questions

As you look around your support group or to persons who have successfully healed, what do they have in common with this list?

What positive attributes do they have that may not be on this list?

Day Three: Watch Your Back

As you celebrate, watch your back.

Satan would take great delight in watching you fall back into the pit. Your self-esteem and body image are his top targets.

Each day we will grow more settled in our new life. As we learn to live in the present, we discover new pleasures in simply living. We don't have to hide our fear anymore, we don't have to suppress grief or shame or anger. We don't have to keep our real selves hidden anymore.

However, our past is still a part of us. We may still be paying the consequences for it (legal or health problems). We may still feel remorse over our actions. We need to remember that our addiction did not simply end because we stopped using our "drug of choice." *We can relapse any time* if we don't keep focused on the Lord *daily* and His Word.

Oswald Chambers asked, "Are you drawing your life from any other source than God Himself? If you are depending upon anything but Him, you will never know when He is gone."[65]

Even though Scripture was written long ago, God's Word is timeless. It is applicable for *us today*. God wants the combination of His steady, constant calling and warm, personal counsel in Scripture to come to characterize *us,* keeping us alert for whatever He will do next (Romans 15:4, Msg).

Healing is active and ongoing. When you finish reading this book, the events described in the book don't end. As we proceed along the path of healing, we make ongoing commitments.

Commitments include developing a strong relationship with

the Lord (relying daily on the Word) and going to support groups or counseling. In other words, we are accountable. If we're afraid to devote ourselves to these commitments, our progress will be blocked. By overcoming our fears, we can move ahead to freedom.

Let's carefully consider our opportunities for growth and not be afraid to make ones that will advance our healing. *Pray for courage and wisdom to make and maintain positive commitments.* Put your armor on everyday and be ready to fight back with "it is written . . ."

Remember that *you are forgiven and deeply loved.*

"Every day you make progress. Every step may be fruitful. Yet there will stretch out before you an ever-lengthening, ever-ascending, ever-improving path. You know you will never get to the end of the journey. But this, so far from discouraging, only adds to the joy of the glory of the climb."

–Sir Winston Churchill, (1874–1965)[66]

☑ Finish these sentences in your journal:

I delight in the fact that my body . . .

Emotionally, I am . . .

Nutritionally, I am . . .

Spiritually, I am . . .

My relationships are . . .

I am . . .

Day Four: Final Instructions

~

Paul gives each of us final instructions.

1 Thessalonians 5:4–24:

⁴ *But, dear brothers, you are not in the dark about these things, and you won't be surprised as by a thief when that day of the Lord comes.* ⁵ *For you are all children of the light and of the day, and do not belong to darkness and night.* ⁶ *So be on your guard, not asleep like the others. Watch for his return and stay sober.* ⁷ *Night is the time for sleep and the time when people get drunk.* ⁸ *But let us who live in the light keep sober, protected by the armor of faith and love, and wearing as our helmet the happy hope of salvation.* ⁹ *For God has not chosen to pour out his anger upon us but to save us through our Lord Jesus Christ;* ¹⁰ *he died for us so that we can live with him forever, whether we are dead or alive at the time of his return.* ¹¹ *So encourage each other to build each other up, just as you are already doing.* ¹² *Dear brothers, honor the officers of your church who work hard among you and warn you against all that is wrong.* ¹³ *Think highly of them and give them your wholehearted love because they are straining to help you. And remember, no quarreling among yourselves.* ¹⁴ *Dear brothers, warn those who are lazy, comfort those who are frightened, take tender care of those who are weak, and be patient with everyone.* ¹⁵ *See that no one pays back evil for evil, but always try to do good to each other and to everyone else.* ¹⁶ *Always be joyful.* ¹⁷ *Always keep on praying.* ¹⁸ *No matter what happens, always be thankful, for this is God's will for you who belong to Christ Jesus.* ¹⁹ *Do not smother the Holy Spirit.* ²⁰ *Do not scoff at those who prophesy,* ²¹ *but test everything that is said to be sure it is true, and if it is, then accept it.* ²² *Keep away from every kind of evil.* ²³ *May the God of peace himself make you entirely pure*

and devoted to God; and may your spirit and soul and body be kept strong and blameless until that day when our Lord Jesus Christ comes back again. [24] *God, who called you to become his child, will do all this for you, just as he promised (TLB).*

> "Healing is learning to trust my own wisdom, my own intuition."
>
> —Unknown

Reflective Questions

As you examined Paul's instructions, what did they mean to you and God's will for you?

Who might be watching your life today, observing your decisions (besides Satan), a person who you can positively impact? Perhaps a younger sister or a friend's daughter that is following the world's ways.

Day Five: Advice from a Friend

$\sim$

Someone will always be prettier or smarter or thinner.

Her house will be bigger. She will drive a better car. Her children will do better in school. Her husband will be more successful than yours. Let it go—love yourself and your circumstances. The prettiest woman in the world can be battling depression. The richest person you know may be lonely. The most envied woman at work may be unable to have children. Speak it out: *I'm not going to compare the inside of me to the outside of her.*

The Word says that if I don't have love, I am nothing. Love who you are right now and let God be your guide. Look in the mirror in the morning and see how much of God you see. *Who's made in God's image? I am!* Love yourself!

It's easy to get discouraged, but remember the woodpecker. He keeps pecking away until he gets the job done! Celebrate, and may God continue to bless you. My motto has become, "When the race ends—the journey begins."

St. Augustine said, "Without us, God will not do certain things, without God, we cannot do them."[67]

☑ **Prayer:** Lord, thank You that my past is past, and that You are doing a new thing in me. Thank You that You have given me a rich future. My heart cries out in joy and thanks for the complete freedom I have in You. Help me live in wholeness and freedom all the days of my life so that You can use me to bring healing to others. And help me always to remember that You have brought me out of Egypt, out of bondage to everything that has ever held me. I am free! You have said so. Alleluia and Amen.

Finale: Week Thirteen

There will be challenges ahead along with many blessings. Keep the words of the prophet Zephaniah close to you always. Zephaniah 3:17–20:

¹⁷For the Lord your God has arrived to live among you. He is a mighty Savior. He will give you victory. He will rejoice over you with great gladness; he will love you and not accuse you. ¹⁸Is that a joyous choir I hear? No, it is the Lord himself exulting over you in happy song. "I have gathered your wounded and taken away your reproach. ¹⁹And I will deal severely with all who have oppressed you. I will save the weak and helpless ones, and bring together those who were chased away. I will give glory to my former exiles, mocked and shamed. ²⁰ At that time, I will gather you together and bring you home again, and give you a good name, a name of distinction among all the peoples of the earth, and they will praise you when I restore your fortunes before your very eyes," says the Lord (TLB).

Promise to Claim: "Do not let this Book of the Law depart from your mouth; meditate on it day and night, so that you may be careful to do everything written in it. Then you will be prosperous and successful" (Joshua 1:8).

Appendix A: Group Leader's Guide

~

Welcome to your new role as a group leader. Maybe you are healed and are being called to minister to others, or perhaps you plan to participate as a member in the group. The following suggestions are given as a guide to leadership and are intended to give you specific ideas for leading the *I'm Beautiful? Why Can't I See It?* devotional study.

The purpose of a healing devotional study group is to provide an opportunity for each woman to discuss the material presented each week in order to develop a greater understanding of themselves and the truth. As you walk through the questions each week, remember that you are trying to help the participants get a broad overview of the major theme of each week. Try not to deal exhaustively with any of the specific topics. Questions that come up for discussion will vary by group, but it is the group leader's job to facilitate and manage the questions and answers.

Some of these topics could take multiple weeks to cover thoroughly, so resist the temptation to give too much time to a single topic or question. This will be your first challenge—to stay on track. Therefore, encourage participants to keep their answers brief. Explain to the group how important it is that they base their answers on God's Word and not on their personal opinions or what their therapist or others say is the truth.

Group leaders should not force anyone to speak. Everyone has the right to say they don't feel comfortable sharing. It takes some women longer than others to feel safe enough to talk. It is also likely that there will be some disagreement on some controversial issues. Some may not agree with certain content. Allow for honest discussion and disagreement. However, encourage people in advance to do so in a spirit of humility and to avoid a spirit of argument.

The goal of the study is not to get people to agree with you and me on every topic, but to get them to think, reflect, and search out the Scripture for themselves, so they can learn to discern the truth for themselves and then take the necessary actions to walk in the truth and apply it to their life.

Support Group

This healing devotional study is not only a Bible study, but it will become a support group for those involved. Your weekly time together is an opportunity to open your hearts and lives to each other and to share how you have been living with, or without, God's Word. It is important to be honest with one another. You will find honesty makes it possible to avoid elements of distress, denial, or discouragement, all of which can hinder a group's progress. It is important to be tolerant and accepting of everyone in the group. The group goal should be to listen and respond from your own experience, strength, and hope.

The group may dredge up some deep-seeded issues. It may cause some to discover that they are not living the abundant life Jesus offers. Some may feel a deep need to reevaluate some of their beliefs. Every person will respond differently. Therefore, group leaders should never make claims concerning a leader's ability or the group's ability to solve a participant's problem. The focus should always remain on Christ and biblical principles.

Every group has a "bleeding-heart." Group leaders should be aware of their limitations. The group leader's role is to stop and show sensitivity to this person, but, at the same time, not allow this person to dominate the group's time. That is your second greatest challenge. If someone is really struggling, you may want to set up another time to meet and talk. *It is important that the group does not turn into a therapy session*—that's why there are therapists! Some participants may need the care of a professional Christian counselor or to speak with their pastor. Pray that the Lord gives you compassion and wisdom as you give direction to the discussion.

Allow the Holy Spirit to work with each person individually. Some people will identify issues that need to be addressed in their lives quickly. For others, it may take time for God to show them what changes they need to make (or for them to find the courage to make those changes). Be patient with your group, and trust God to work with each person in His way and His time. Remember, the Holy Spirit directed this person to the group—the Holy Spirit will work in this person.

Writing Assignments

There are a number of exercises that require writing in a journal. For example, in Week Six, each team member is asked to write a separate letter to each person they are angry with and share one of those letters with the group. They should write the letter in their spare time, not during the class. It can follow the suggested format, or they can create their own letter. They are asked to do this again in Week Nine (forgiveness letters).

Confidentiality

Explain during the first session of the group that there is a policy of confidentiality. What is discussed in the group should not be mentioned outside the group. I have each person in the group sign a form agreeing to this.

Preparing for Each Meeting

As the group leader, you need to be doing the study along

with your group. Make sure each person has her or his own study guide and Bible. This study primarily uses the New International Version (NIV). Remind each person that this is a commitment towards restoration, and it is important to commit *at least* twenty to thirty minutes a day to the study.

Encourage group members to be consistent and not get behind with their homework. If they keep up, they will get much more out of the class. But remember, everyone has different schedules, priorities, and works at her or his own pace. Some will not have a chance to do all of their homework. For this reason, you may find some people will want to go through this study a second time.

Let everyone know that even if they don't get their homework done, they are welcome. It's more important that they hear God's Word and fellowship, rather than answer each question.

Structure and Format

ABC's:
A—Always begin on time.
B—Be committed: Make this time a weekly priority.
C—Confidentiality: Everything shared in the group stays in the group.

The ideal time frame for the group is one and a half to two hours. For example, with of group of eight people or less, I can read through an entire week's material and discuss each question in two hours. When the group is eight or more, I want to give everyone an opportunity to speak. I will divide the time available by the number of people in the group. I ask each one to bring out something meaningful or life changing to them from the week's study. I encourage them to share answers to the reflective questions and allow them to ask questions or express concerns.

Group Discussion Format

The group discussion is intended to be an overview of the topic and includes questions. Depending on how much time you have, the size of your group, and how verbal your group is, you may pick and choose which questions you want to discuss. They don't necessarily have to come from the book.

Start and end the session with prayer. You can either pray as a group or break out into pairs (I suggest this if you have a large group). Idea: You may want to have each woman write out her prayer request for the week on an index card (you will need to supply index cards). Each person passes the card to another person, so that each person is praying for someone specifically each week.

Long Term Success

For this to be a successful ministry long term, this will need the same priority given to other important ministries of the church. Try to recruit leaders that participate in the groups. In addition, there may be certain leaders within the church that will feel led to become a group leader. The more leaders that go through the groups, the fewer people will believe that the groups are only for those who are "really having problems." Try not to *label* this ministry. People will resist attending groups where they are labeled.

Promote the study as a positive experience appropriate for anyone concerned about body image or issues with food.

I pray that as you take on this very important role, God will give you wisdom and insight to help the people in your group understand and embrace important truths that you will be discussing.

Teamwork is important. There is strength in numbers. Without the team approach, helpers are likely to become overburdened. After your group leaders gain experience, reach out to your community to meet people hurting with emotional eating. It may take some time to start a healing ministry for people with disordered eating and negative body image. Many will take the "wait and see" approach. Be optimistic. Don't quit!

God promises that if we seek Him, we will find Him. His Word is the greatest power for change in the entire universe. You will see lives changed through this study, including your own. God has the power to set us free from bondage so that we may live a joyful, abundant life.

My prayer is that you will experience His presence, His grace, His love, and His Truth in a mighty powerful way as you lead each group. May God richly bless your efforts!

Appendix B: Guidelines for Prayer and Meditation

~

If you pray right, your prayers are answered. If you pray wrong, they're answered too.

Praying right is praying daily for help from our emotional eating issues coupled with gratitude for the help received. God is unlimited in His ability and desire to bless our life and answer our prayers. As we continue to honor the Lord, we will see miraculous things take place in our life. We trust and praise Him for His loving kindness. The wisdom and guidance contained in God's Word is available to us any time, day or night.

As children, we learned to say *please* and *thank you*. The first prayer of the day should be *please* for help and healing, and our last prayer at night should be *thank you* for the progress we made. Expressing gratitude each day, all day, opens our hearts to be nourished by His love.

Prayer and meditation are inseparable and are our principal means of contact (communication) with God. It is the way we establish our desire to do God's will. Prayer is speaking to God, whereas meditation is listening to God. We ask God to reveal His will to us through His Word, the Bible. We listen for an answer (in everything we do). The reward is strength, wisdom, and peace of mind.

> "Our ears might become satisfied with hearing; but God's ears are never satisfied. He is never wearied by our prayers."
> –Jewish Midrash

An Overview of Prayer and Meditation

Prayer: The act of making a reverent petition, or act of communion to God, such as in devotion, confession, praise, or thanksgiving.[68] Praising God helps us grow and change. Praying for knowledge of God's will and the ability to obey His will is important for healing.

Meditation: Is often misunderstood as some difficult, mysterious practice used by monks or mystics. Christian meditation is different from Eastern meditation. The meditation of the Eastern religion relies on emptying the mind of conscious thought. Christian meditation is the discipline of growing in your knowledge of God by studying the Bible and the attributes and acts of God. We listen for God's answer. The Bible urges us to meditate on who God is, what He has done, and what He has said.

Meditation is simply focused thinking: A skill you can learn and use anywhere. When you think about a problem over and over, that's *worry.* When you think about God's Word over and over, that's *meditation.* If you know how to worry—you know how to meditate! Just switch your attention to Bible verses. When applied to our current circumstances, these Bible lessons can change our lives.

Listening to God

Prayer can be a two-way conversation. We can actively listen to God. Personally, I ask God to quiet me enough so that I can listen. I ask God to speak to me, and then I wait. God will talk to us not just in the quiet times but also in the middle of the noise, and the trick is to hear Him through the noise.

Appendix C: Thorn or Addiction?

~

- Substance Abuse
- Alcohol and Illegal Drug Abuse
- Abortion
- Self-harm
- Violence
- Demonic Influences

> "Addiction is answering the spiritual calling inside us by go-
> ing to the wrong address."
>
> –Anonymous

Congratulations for completing the study! As you scan the topic list above, do you see another area of your life where you are held captive? Many of you will zoom in on at least one of the topics. This chapter is intended to provide information to enable you to fight these other demons so that you may truly find complete healing and restoration. A resource list can be found in Appendix E.

Where can we go to feel better, to feel spiritually alive? Not to overeating, alcohol, or other drugs. When we turn to these things to feel better, we're trading one addiction for another. Some of us have an addictive-compulsive personality and struggle with either "dual addictions" (involves food plus alcohol and/or chemical substances), or "musical addictions." That's when we quit one bad habit and substitute it with another one. We want to avoid musical addictions. The solution: Invite God to fill the void in our souls, and ask Him to help us find healthy alternatives. For example, I swapped food bingeing for designing personalized "Auntie Kim" dolls. That has been the objective of this study—to give you the God-tools to fill the voids.

Thorn or Addiction?

An addiction is an overwhelming urge to fill our emptiness with an object, such as food (or alcohol, substances, sex). It is anything that masters a person's life. The apostle Paul writes, "Everything is permissible for me—but not everything is beneficial. Everything is permissible for me—but I will not be mastered by anything" (1 Corinthians 6:12). What Paul is saying is just because something is technically legal (like rich foods, diet pills, alcohol, tobacco), that doesn't mean that it's spiritually suitable.

What is a thorn? An encyclopedia says, "A sharp, pointed projection (on some plants), usually protective in function."[69] A dictionary says, "Something that causes distress or irritation."[70] According to Dr. R. T. Kendall, author of *A Thorn in the Flesh,* it may be a personal weakness, handicap, unhappy employment, or financial hardship. We all have thorns. Why would a loving God severely chasten His children with a thorn in the flesh? Kendall says that God gets our attention through these thorns. Some thorns may never go away, but God's grace is sufficient to handle them for life.[71]

"For all we know about thorns, we can be sure of this God would prefer we have an occasional limp than a perpetual strut. And if it takes a thorn for Him to make His point, he loves us enough not to pluck it out."

—Max Lucado, *In the Grip of Grace*[72]

Substance Abuse

Substance abuse is an addiction. Your thorn may be vanity,

which, when taken to extremes, leads to the addiction of diet pills, laxatives, and diuretics. Perhaps you've never thought of yourself as a substance abuser because these are legal products that are available over the counter. The words "substance abuse" conjures up the image of the rundown, homeless heroin addict. I smoked cigarettes. I ingested thousand's of laxative, diuretic, caffeine, and diet pills. Those are substances. It is substance abuse when you don't follow the recommended dosage.

Laxative Abuse

Laxative abuse is the most prevalent, and stopping the cycle has proven difficult for many. People who abuse laxatives often find themselves in a no-win situation. They use laxatives to "feel thin," which is an immediate, positive result. Eventually, the opposite occurs. They find themselves "feeling fat" from excessive water retention (a delayed, negative result). *How do I stop abusing laxatives?* [73]

Stop taking laxatives right now. Do not take any more unless your physician instructs you to. Stimulant-type laxatives are especially harmful to the body.

Drink at least six to ten cups of water a day. Do not drink caffeinated beverages, because they act like a diuretic, promoting loss of fluid. Restricting your fluid intake promotes dehydration and worsens constipation.

Include daily physical activity to regulate your bowel function. Discuss the intensity and type of activity with your health care provider. Too much or too vigorous exercise can worsen constipation due to the effects on your metabolism and fluid balance.

Eat regularly. It is important that you spread the amount of food across at least three meals a day. Eat these meals at regular intervals.

Eat foods that promote normal bowel movements, like whole-grain breads, cereals, crackers, vegetables, fruits, and foods with wheat bran added. Prunes and prune juice are not recommended because the ingredient in prunes that promotes bowel movements is actually an irritant laxative. Long-term use of prunes and prune juice can result in the same problem as long-term use of laxatives.

Write down the frequency of your bowel movements. If you are constipated for more than three days, call your healthcare provider.

Laxative Withdrawal

There is no way to predict exactly how stopping laxatives will affect you. The amount or length of time laxatives have been used is not an indicator of how severe the withdrawal symptoms will be.

Common side effects of laxative withdrawal are constipation, fluid retention, feeling bloated, and temporary weight gain. You can see that laxative withdrawal is especially difficult for people with emotional eating. If you are still highly reactive to feeling fat, the symptoms of laxative withdrawal may worsen this feeling.

To help you get through the process of laxative withdrawal, *it is essential to remember that any weight gain associated with laxative withdrawal is only temporary.* Symptoms of laxative withdrawal do *not* lead to permanent weight gain.

How long will laxative withdrawal last? This varies greatly. Most people have symptoms for one to three weeks after stopping laxatives.

Alcohol and Illegal Drug Abuse

I struggled with bulimia for sixteen years. During that time, I was a binge drinker. If I was loaded, I could be someone else. I couldn't go out on a date or go to party without getting loaded for fear someone might see *the real me*. It is not uncommon for those of us struggling with disordered eating to also be addicted to alcohol or illegal substances.

If you walk into an AA meeting, chances are there are a few in the group with an eating disorder. It's becomes a matter of discerning which substance has greater control over your life. The bottom line is in order to live a healthy, non-addictive lifestyle, all addictions must be dealt with, and this study has been designed to give you the necessary God-tools. Or perhaps you live with a substance abuser. God willing, that person will see the incredible change in you and desire the same thing (Jesus).

Abortion

There are many women who, while in the midst of their addiction, made a choice to have an abortion. Left unresolved, this event will be a thorn for life. I was one of those women. There are other women who have had an abortion and disordered eating is triggered from the event. In a survey conducted by Open Arms Ministry, eighty percent of post-abortive women reported problems with guilt, while seventy percent reported depression. Sixty-three percent said they couldn't forgive themselves.[74]

Many of us who have had an abortion repress feelings of guilt, shame, anger, and grief. We feel we have bigger monsters to slay. An abortion is a *big* monster, whether you have dealt with it yet or not. If you don't think it is a monster, God does. One of the things that *God despises* is "hands that shed innocent blood" (Proverbs 6:17). Therefore, it is necessary to come to terms with this event before God. Let me share my story with you.

Many years ago, I found myself pregnant. I had a choice—to bring the baby to term or abort it. There was no doubt in my mind that abortion was the answer. After all, I wasn't married, I had an established career and lifestyle, and the father wasn't a significant other. My family physician offered resources and I replied, "Just give me the contact information. I'll take care of it." I did take care of "it," then proceeded to erase the incident from my memory bank.

Two years later, I accepted Jesus Christ as my Lord and Savior. I became keenly aware of the sin I had committed, a sin that God has graciously and mercifully forgiven. Even as a Christian, I never thought of that baby or the abortion again. That was until a couple of years ago.

As I was navigating through a women's Bible study, my abortion experience surfaced. I felt an intense pressure to make a choice. I could rebury this event away forever, or I could turn to God and ask Him to shine His bright light on this dark situation. I chose the latter, the right choice. With God's guidance, I began to retrieve the data from the bottom of the ocean where I had so carefully buried it.

I signed up for a post-abortal Bible study and support group (Healing Encouragement for Abortion Related Trauma). Class didn't start for a few weeks, and I began to question the choices I made years earlier. I wanted answers to some questions that had been plaguing me. *Father, tell me, show me what was I feeling when I was pregnant for those eight weeks. I don't have any memory of what was going through my mind or what was on my heart. Nothing! You know everything. You were there. Please show me.* I got my answer. An answer I wasn't prepared for.

At the time of my pregnancy, I was living with that monster, bulimia. Binging and purging was my life. I made a choice that day, a choice to *purge* my baby. To me, that's what the baby was—a blob of tissue that could be purged away, like the food I ate and my body fluids. I could clearly see that at that time in my life, I didn't value myself, so how could I value my baby's life? You could say this monster took two innocent lives.

As God started revealing details, I began putting together the story. I had found many reasons to justify my actions. The truth is I was just plain selfish. I was more concerned about my body and what other people would think of me than for a human life. *They* told me it was a blob of tissue only an inch long. They were right, it was an inch long, but I learned later that this developing life was already termed a fetus (Latin for *young one*).

Everything was present in that fetus that was found in a fully developed adult. The heart had been beating for more than a month, the stomach was producing digestive juices, and the kidneys had begun to function. Forty muscle sets had begun to operate in conjunction with the nervous system. The fetus body responded to the touch from the physician before he/she was aborted.[75]

God had a great plan for this little person's life, and I made the wrong choice. *No, I was not justified!* Then I became angry . . . then remorseful. Through God's mercy and counsel, I was able to forgive myself.

I was forgiven and set free because I made the right choice. Everything has consequences. It is at a time like this that our loving, compassionate Father draws us close and whispers love and hope into our heart and soul. In quiet times of meditation, we can learn to listen to the inner voice that guides us to satisfying choices.

I learned a great deal about myself as I healed from bulimia but found it necessary and advantageous to explore and heal from the effects of my abortion. I encourage anyone who has had an abortion to take a post-abortion Bible study class or church-related study. You will meet and bond with some exceptional women.

Self-Harm

The act of deliberately hurting yourself falls under the terms of *self-harm, self-injury, and self-mutilation.* Today, more than six million adolescents are mutilating themselves with razors, glass, knives, and nails.[76] Many people who self-harm do not even know they are doing it. For example, some people pinch themselves until they bleed or pull out their hair or pick at their toenails and/or fingernails until they bleed.

Self-harm, like disordered eating, indicates that you didn't learn healthy ways of coping with overwhelming feelings. You're not disgusting or sick; you never learned positive ways to deal with your feelings. Many say when they "cut," they don't feel pain.

They feel relief. Self-harm, like disordered eating, may also give a feeling of being in control of one's own body, which can be especially important for victims of sexual abuse.

> "Cut me open, watch me bleed, let the brokenness be seen. Let it out, those words you just can't say. Let it heal and do it another day."
>
> —Anonymous

Did you know self-harm has been going on for centuries? When you have time, read Mark 5:1–20, the healing of a demon-possessed man. It's the story about a man who lived like an animal in the tombs. Scripture says that "night and day among the tombs and in the hills *he would cry out and cut himself with stones*" (5:5). Perhaps he did this to see if he could bleed, to try to feel if anything was left alive in him.

Violence

Most Americans tend to underestimate the extent of sexual or domestic violence and are unaware of the factors that place women at risk.

- One out of three women worldwide is affected by violence.
- Battering is the leading cause of injury in women in the USA, more than rape, muggings, and traffic accidents combined.[77]
- Nearly two million women are physically assaulted every year. The Bureau of Justice's National Crime Survey reports that a woman is battered in her home every fifteen seconds (The Battered Woman's Survival Guide, 4).
- One out of every four women on college campuses has been a victim of rape or attempted rape.
- Almost one-half of all immigrant women experience some kind of domestic violence.

Many women (and some men) believe they deserve to be treated and hurt this way. They believe whole-heartedly that violence is a thorn that they must endure. There is nothing further from the truth, as we learned in "Week Four: Seeking the Truth." Any person who is being harmed can take action.

Violence is *never* your fault. There is no sure way to prevent it, but there are ways to reduce the risk:

Trust your instincts and act immediately. If you don't feel safe or comfortable in a particular situation or environment, *leave.*

Avoid individuals who don't respect you or your decisions.

Do not mix sexual decisions with drugs and alcohol.

Learn which behaviors constitute sexual violence and domestic violence. When you're on a date, never feel you "owe" that person something.

Use the buddy system; walk with a friend.

Walk near the curb. Avoid being alone in isolated areas, such as dark doorways, parking lots, and garages.

If you're out having drinks, do not leave your glass unattended. Be alert at all times. Guard against someone spiking your drink with drugs that will make you unconscious and an easy target for a rapist.

When going out with someone new, consider taking along some friends and/or meeting in a public place.

Before you get into your car, have your keys ready and check the backseat.

If you think someone is following you, call for assistance and/or run toward a public place.[78]

> "Never confuse a single defeat with a final defeat."
> –F. Scott Fitzgerald, Author (1896–1940)

Demonic Influences

When I first heard the term "demonic influences," I conjured up visions of witches casting spells over a foggy tub of brew. But many counselors help patients identify areas in their lives where there may be demonic influences or oppression.

Mary Magdalene was a tormented woman before she met Jesus. Jesus had set Mary free from seven demons (Mark 16:9). When Jesus found Mary, He saw a woman in trouble. How could He bring peace to such a tormented woman? We don't know exactly what happened in her life to bring on her despair (the seven demons). Perhaps she was abused as a child or suffered horrible heartache? How did she become so plagued by Satan? Maybe Mary wanted to cry out for help, but she wanted to keep everyone at a distance because she thought no one could help her. No one could . . . until Jesus.

Perhaps you feel oppressed by Satan. Seek the Word. "If we confess our sins, he is faithful and just and will forgive us our sins and purify us from all unrighteousness" (1 John 1:9–10). Once we confess our sins, receive the Lord's forgiveness and cleansing, then we can pray in the name of Jesus Christ to break the power of any demonic influence or control. Remember, "It is written . . . It is written . . ."

The Thorn Bird

There is a legend about a bird, the thorn bird, which sings just once in its life more sweetly than any other creature on the face of the earth. From the moment it leaves the nest, it searches for a thorn tree and does not rest until it has found one. Then, singing among the savage branches, it impales itself upon the longest, sharpest spine. Dying, it rises above its own agony to outcarol the lark and the nightingale. One superlative song. Existence the price. The whole world stills to listen, and God in heaven smiles. For the best is only bought at the cost of great pain . . . or so says the legend.[79]

Where have we heard a similar story—about a man who bought the best for us at the cost of great pain?

Appendix D: Finding a Healthy Church Community

~

As you continue to grow into a deeper relationship with the Father, Son, and Holy Spirit, you will need to nourish this relationship and keep watering your beautiful garden with the knowledge and grace of God. Finding a healthy church to worship with is critical and challenging.

Searching for a (new) church is never easy because churches are made up of broken people. It is important to emphasize that a healthy church does not mean a church is composed of only healthy people.

Despite the hurdles, if you pour a great deal of prayer into each step and each visit you make, you can find a place to call home.

What Does A Healthy Church Look Like?

The Scriptures describe important aspects and elements to look for when choosing a church today. Look at the earliest church:

[42] They devoted themselves to the apostles' teaching and to the fellowship, to the breaking of bread and to prayer. [46] Every day they continued to meet together in the temple courts. They broke bread in their homes and ate together with glad and sincere hearts, [47] praising God and enjoying the favor of all the people. And the Lord added to their number daily those who were being saved (Acts 2:42, 46–47).

Bible Food

We are told that "All Scripture is God-breathed and is useful for teaching, rebuking, correcting and training in righteousness, so that the man of God may be thoroughly equipped for every good work" (2 Timothy 3:16–17).

Questions to ask are:

- Is the Bible accepted as the authoritative Word of God?
- Are the members being fed genuine Bible food?
- Does the pastor or minister use the Bible to teach?

Look for a church where truth is preached from the Bible, where God's Word is seen as living, relevant, changeless, and inerrant, rather than just a "good book" filled with advice on how to be a more loving, moral person. Look for a church where difficult passages, as well as straightforward ones, are preached with clarity.

Fellowship

We all want a church where we feel welcomed, a place to belong. Does this church "make every effort to keep the unity of the Spirit through the bond of peace" (Ephesians 4:3)? What does a warm and welcoming church look like?

- People in the seats around you introduce themselves before or after the services.
- The pastor or a visitation team offers to visit you.
- People your age invite you to participate in events.
- The church meets adult special needs through ministry opportunities such as discipleship studies, new believers, Christian studies, divorce and grief recovery groups, 12-step programs, and other opportunities to integrate the *unchurched* into the community. Childcare should be available so you may attend these groups.

Fit

Finding a good fit can be more challenging than you think. Today, there is a wide variety of churches to choose from, and each one has differences:

Stylistic: Do you like contemporary worship? Old-time hymns? Gospel songs? Worship choruses? With or without percussion, organ, or live orchestra? Worship isn't simply about meeting a style preference or eliciting a purely emotional response within the worshiper; its purpose is to focus on and glorify God.

Structural: How are decisions made? Collectively or by a leadership board? Look for a leadership structure that you agree with.

Doctrinal: All believers should learn what is essential for them in the Christian faith. Pray for discernment.

Historical: Are you going to this church because your family has always been members (but you are bored to death)?

The right "fit" is like a pair of blue jeans. They're comfortable. It's important to feel comfortable, whether that means wearing those comfortable blue jeans or feeling feminine in a dress and hat. If you are not comfortable where you worship, then every little thing becomes a problem, a thorn, and God doesn't get any of the glory.

Bear Fruit

Serving God and others may be a new concept to you, but it was the attitude of the New Testament church. Jesus himself said: "It is more blessed to give than to receive" (Acts 20:35).

Week Three, Day Four we talked about "Divine Pruning." You are in a good church when your life bears good fruit (John 15:1–8). God gives each one of us gifts and talents for use in building His church. Often, it takes initiative from the pastoral or ministry staff to help a newcomer fit into ministry and begin to bear fruit.

A church has opportunities for you to serve when:

- You observe in the bulletin ministries that fit your spiritual gifts and interests.
- You contact a ministry leader about your interest to serve and receive a concrete, welcoming invitation to participate.
- A ministry leader actually initiates contact with you to invite you to participate in a new or ongoing ministry of the church.
- Find yourself serving God in ways that are compatible with your gifts, talents, and unique personality.

Convenience and Location

Your church should be located within a distance convenient enough for you to feel you have the opportunity to get plugged in, be an active member rather than just a Sunday attendee. A church is convenient when:

- Driving to an evening or midweek event doesn't leave you exhausted.
- A church small-group meeting is located in your neighborhood or community.
- Your children see some of the church children at their school.

Closing Moments

There are no perfect churches because there are no perfect people (refer to Week Two). Seek a church community where grace is lived and you can feel and see God's grace in the members. I've heard too many horror stories of a recovered person seeking a new church family only to be condemned and ridiculed for their past or the way they looked, feeding feelings of worthlessness. This is not Christ-like behavior and serves as an example of why it is important to take the time to do your homework and try several churches before settling in.

Find a church that builds self-respect and dignity and promotes surrender and trust in the Lord Jesus Christ. A church set in forgiveness, grace, and unconditional love. A church that clearly preaches the Word of God and helps you find your purpose. God bless you on this new journey, and pray, pray, pray!

Appendix E: Resources

Organizations and General Referrals

American Association of Christian Counselors [www.aacc.net]; P.O. Box 739 Forest, VA 24551. 1–434–525–9470

Association of Christian Therapists (ACT); 14440 Cherry Lane Court #215 Laurel, MD 10707. 1–301–470-ACTS

National Association for Christian Recovery [www.christianrecovery.com]; P.O. Box 215, Brea, CA 92822–0215. 1–714–529–6227

Suicide: National Suicide Hope Line. 1–800–784–2433

Abortion

Care Net [www.care-net.org]; 109 Carpenter Drive, Sterling, Virginia 20164. 1–703–478–5661. E-mail Care Net to find locations near you: info@care-net.org

Elliot Institute [www.afterabortion.org]; PO Box 7348, Springfield, IL 62791–7348. 1–217–525–8202

Focus on the Family [www.family.org]; Colorado Springs, CO, 80995. 1–800-A FAMILY

National Office of Post-Abortion Reconciliation (Catholic organization) "Project Rachel" [www.hopeafterabortion.com]

Rachel's Vineyard (Catholic focus) [www.rachelsvineyard.org]; 877–467–3463

Ramah International [www.ramahinternational.org]; 866–807–2624

Safe Haven Ministries [www.postabortionpain.com]; P.O. Box 336 Beardstown, IL 62618

Alcohol

Alcoholics Anonymous (AA) [www.alcoholics-anonymous.org]; AA World Services, Inc., P.O. Box 459, New York, NY 10163. Check the website for local chapters.

Alcoholics Victorious [av.iugm.org]; Association of Gospel Rescue Missions, 1045 Swift Street, Kansas City, MO 64116. 1–816–471–8020

Al-Anon Family Group Headquarters, Inc. [www.al-anon.org]; 1600 Corporate Landing Pkwy., Virginia Beach, VA 23454–5617. 1–888–425–2666

Christian Alcoholics Rehabilitation Association; FOA Road Pocahontas, Mississippi 39072

Addiction

Twelve Steps to Freedom for Alcohol and Drug Abuse; 3100 S.E. 68th Ave. #19, Camas, WA 98607. 1–360–944–1296

Christians in Recovery [www.christians-in-recovery.org]; P.O. Box 4422 Tequesta, FL 33469. A ministry to those struggling with addiction to substances, sex, weight control, and domestic abuse.

Overcomers Outreach [www.overcomersoutreach.org]; P.O. Box 2208, Oakhurst, CA 93644. 1–800–310–3001

For Adolescents: S.A.F.E. [www.safeorlando.com]; 5607 Hansel Avenue, Orlando, FL 32809. 407–812–8680

Check with your local Rescue Mission organization. Many across the country have long-term recovery programs for men and women that are free of charge.

Disordered Eating

Overeaters Anonymous [www.overeatersanonymous.org]; World Service Office 6075 Zenith Court NE, Rio Rancho, New Mexico 87124–6424. Check your phone book for local chapters in your area.

The American Anorexia/Bulimia Association, Inc., 293 Central Park West, New York, NY 10024. 1–212–501–8351

National Eating Disorders Association [www.nationaleatingdisorders.org]; 603 Stewart St., Suite 803, Seattle, WA 98101. 1–206–382–3587

National Association of Anorexia Nervosa and Associated Disorders [www.altrue.net/site/anadweb]; Box 7, Highland Park, IL 60035. 1–847- 831–3438

Eating Disorder Referral and Information Center [www.edreferral.com]

Focus on the Family [www.family.org], Colorado Springs, CO 80920. 1–800-A FAMILY

FamilyLife [www.familylife.com]; P.O. Box 7111, Little Rock, AR 72223. 1–800–358–6329

Disordered Eating Treatment Centers

Remuda Ranch [www.remudaranch.com]; One East Apache StreetWickenburg, AZ 85390. 1–800–445–1900

Mercy Ministries of America [www.mercyministries.com]; PO Box 111060, Nashville, TN 37222–1060. 1–615- 831–6987. Mercy Ministries does not charge for their services, but that there a long wait list.

Canopy Cove [www.canopycove.com] 2300 Killearn Center Blvd., Tallahassee, FL 32309. 1–800–236–7524

Minirth-Meier New Life Clinics [www.meiernewlifeclinics.com]; 1–888–7CLINIC. Refer to website to locate a clinic near you.

A Place of Hope [www.aplaceofhope.com]; Edmond, WA. 1–888–771–5166

Violence (Battery, Rape, Abuse)

National Domestic Violence Hotline [http://www.ndvh. org]; 1–800–799-SAFE (7233)

National Sexual Assault Hotline [http://www.nsvrc.org]; 1–800–656–4673

National Child Abuse Hotline; 1–800–422–4453

Family Violence Prevention Fund [http://www.endabuse. org]; 1–415–252–8900

Rape, Abuse and Incest National Network [http://www. rainn.org]; 1–800–656-HOPE

National Center for Victims of Crime [http://www.ncvc. org]; **1–800–211–7996**

Resources

Abortion

Cochrane, Linda. *Forgiven and Set Free;* Grand Rapids: Baker Books. 1996, Care Net

Alcorn, Randy. *Why ProLife?* Sisters: Multnomah Publishers Inc. 2005

Anger and Forgiveness

Seamonds, Dave. *Healing For Damaged Emotions;* Colorado Springs: Cook Communications. 1991.

Carter, Les. *Choosing to Forgive Workbook;* Nashville: Thomas Nelson. 1997.

Minirth, Frank and Carter, Les. *The Anger Workbook for Christian Parents;* Hoboken: John Wiley & Sons. 2004

Stanley, Charles. *The Gift of Forgiveness;* Nashville: Thomas Nelson. 2002.

Depression

Jantz, Gregory L. *Moving Beyond Depression;* New York: Random House, Inc. 2003

Lucado, Max. *God Came Near;* Sisters: Multnomah Publishers Inc. 1995

Dillow, Linda. *Calm My Anxious Heart;* Colorado Springs: NavPress. 1998.

Disordered Eating, Healing, and Self-Worth

Jantz, Gregory L. *Hope, Help and Healing for Eating Disorders;* Colorado Springs: Waterbook Press. 2002.

McGee, Robert S. *The Search for Significance: Getting a Glimpse of Your True Worth Through God's Eyes (Revised);* Nashville: Thomas Nelson. 2003.

Anderson, N., Gerzon F., & King, J.E. *Released From Bondage;* Nashville: Thomas Nelson. 2002

Cloud, Henry. *Changes That Heal: How To Understand Your Past to Ensure a Healthier Future;* Grand Rapids: Zondervan. 1992

Fitzpatrick, Elyse. *Love to Eat, Hate to Eat: Breaking the Bondage of Destructive Eating Habits;* Eugene: Harvest House Publishers. 2005

Luce, Katie. *The Pursuit of Beauty;* Green Forest: New Leaf Press. 1997

Hersh, Sharon. *Mom, I Feel Fat!* New York: Random House, Inc. 2001

Homme, Martha. *Seeing Yourself in God's Image—Overcoming Anorexia and Bulimia (Workbook);* Available through Turning Point Ministries. 1–800–879–4770. Chatanooga: Turning Point. 2001.

Mintle, Linda. *Getting Unstuck,* Lake Mary: Creation House. 2000.

Alcorn, Nancy. *Mercy For Eating Disorders;* Franklin: Providence House. 2003.

McGee, Robert and Mountcastle, William Drew. *Conquering Eating Disorders (workbook),* Nashville: LifeWay Press. 1994.

Bevere, Lisa. *You Are Not What You Weigh;* Lake Mary: Creation House. 1998.

Keller, Kay, et al. *Hand in Hand: Devotions for Encouraging Families Through the Pain of a Daughter with an Eating Disorder.* Phoenix: Ironwood Lithographers. 1998.

McClure, Cynthia Roland. *The Monster Within: Facing An Eating Disorder;* Grand Rapids: Baker Book House. 2002.

Wilson, Nancy M. *In Pursuit of the Ideal: Finding Your Identity and Living in True Freedom;* Orlando: NewLife Publications. 2003.

Food and Nutrition

The Center for Counseling and Health Resources, Inc.

Gregory L. Jantz, "Hope, Help and Healing for Eating Disorders, *The Power of Nutrition*"; Wheaton: Harold Shaw Publishers. 1995

Gregory Jantz, *The Total Temple Makeover,* West Monroe: Howard Publishing. 2005

"A Place of Hope" online store provides Specialized Nutritional Supplements for those suffering with an eating disorder. Visit: www.aplaceofhope.com

Yphantides, Nick, M.D., *HealthSteward.com* [http://www.healthsteward.com]

Mintle, Linda. *Breaking Free From Compulsive Overeating;* Lake Mary: Charisma House. 2002.

Purpose: God's Plan for You

Warren, Rick. *The Purpose Driven Life:* Grand Rapids: Zondervan. 2002.

Blackaby, Henry & King, Claude V. *Experiencing God: Knowing and Doing the Will of God;* Nashville: LifeWay Press. 1990.

Self-Harm: Websites

Communicating with the Self-Injurer (From Self-Injury Support)

[http://www.sisupport.org/communicating_with_si.htm]

Family and Friends (From Self-Injury: A Struggle)

[http://www.self-injury.net/familyandfriends]

Helpful Responses to Self-injury (From Bristol Crisis Service for Women)

[http://www.users.zetnet.co.uk/BCSW/leaflets/helpresp.
htm]

Help for Families and Friends (From Secret Shame):
[http://www.palace.net/~llama/psych/ffriend.html]

Suffering

Elliot, Elisabeth. *A Path Through Suffering: Discovering the Relationship Between God's Mercy and Our Pain;* Delight: Gospel Light.

Bridges, Jerry. *Trusting God Even When Life Hurts;* Colorado Springs: NavPress. 1990.

Dobson, James. *When God Doesn't Make Sense;* Carol Stream: Tyndale House. 1993.

Kreeft; Peter. *Making Sense Out of Suffering;* Cincinnati: St. Anthony Messenger Press. 1986.

Yancey, Philip. *Where Is God When It Hurts;* Grand Rapids: Zondervan. 1997.

Tada, Joni Eareckson & Estes, Steven. *When God Weeps;* Grand Rapids: Zondervan. 2002.

Arthur, Kay. *Lord, Where Are You When Bad Things Happen?* New York: Random House. 2000.

Arthur, Kay. *Lord Heal My Hurts,* Colorado Springs: Waterbook Press. 2000. (Bible Study)

Sittser, Gerald L. *A Grace Disguised: How the Soul Grows Through Loss;* Grand Rapids: Zondervan. 1996.

Endnotes

1 Rivers, Francine. 2004. Keynote Speaker, Oregon Christian Writers Summer Conference, 1 August 2004.

2 Partow Donna, *Becoming the Woman I Want to* Be, Minneapolis:Bethany House Publishers, 2004

3 http://www.christians-in-recovery.com; accessed January 2005

41 & 2 Cited by Parham, A. Philip. 1993. Body, Mind and Soul, 1045, *Recovery Devotional Bible,* Grand Rapids: Zondervan.

5 Packer, J.I., *Knowing God,* 129. Downers Grove: InterVarsity Press, 1993

6 Chambers, Oswald. 1963.Vision and Darkness, *My Utmost for His Highest,* January 19, Uhrichville: Barbour and Company.

7 Ninon de l'Enclos Quotes; http://www.brainyquote.com/quotes/quotes/n/ninondele120260.html; accessed December, 2004

8 Gribble, Kenneth. *The Plain Truth,* September-October 2004

9 Stafford, Nancy, *Beauty By The Book,* 148, Sisters: Multonomah, 2002

10 Graham, Ruth Bell, *Women's Devotional Bible 2, NIV,* Weekending: Realize, 14, Grand Rapids: Zondervan. 1995.

11 Jantz, Gregory L. 1995. *Hope, Help, and Healing for Eating Disorders,* 63, Wheaton: Harold Shaw Publishers.

12 Quoted: *Women's Devotional Bible,* 524, Grand Rapids: Zondervan. 1995.

13 Mason, Mike, *The Gospel According To Job,* 141, Wheaton: Crossway Books, 1994

14 *The American Heritage Dictionary of the English Language, Fourth Edition; Houghton Mifflin Company, 2000*

15 Parham, A. Philip, *Recovery Devotional Bible,* Grand Rapids: Zondervan, 1984

16 Sheila Walsh, *The Heartache No One Sees,* 173, Nashville: Thomas Nelson, 2004

17 Newman, Deborah, *Loving Your Body,* 21–22, Wheaton: Tyndale House, 2002.

18 Aburdine, Patricia and Naisbitt, John. *Megatrends for Women,* 322, New York: Villard Books, 1992.

19 Stafford, Nancy, *Beauty By The Book,* 119, Sisters: Multonomah, 2002

20 *The American Heritage Dictionary of the English Language, Fourth Edition, 2000 by Houghton Mifflin Company*

21 Paraphrased, Screwtape *Letters* by C.S. Lewis: Severson, Beth Donignon. 1995. *Women's Devotional Bible 2, NIV,* 1274, Grand Rapids: Zondervan

22 Crabb, Larry and Allender, Dan B., *Hope When Your're Hurting,* 103, Grand Rapids: Zondervan, 1996

23 Stanley, Charles F. 2004. *In Touch, January 2005,* 27, Atlanta: In Touch Ministries.

24 http://en.wikipedia.org/wiki/Gallup%27s_List_of_Widely_Admired_People

25 Crabb, Larry, & Allender, Dan. 1996. *Hope When You're Hurting,* 106–107, Grand Rapids: Zondervan Publishing House.

26 Lucado, Max. 2004. *In the Grip of Grace,* http://www.Christians-In-Recovery.com, December 14, 2004.

27 Stafford, Nancy, *Beauty By The Book,* 75, Sisters: Multonomah, 2002

28 *The American Heritage Dictionary of the English Language, Fourth Edition, Houghton Mifflin Company, 2000*

29 Jantz, Gregory L. 1995. *Hope, Help, and Healing for Eating Disorders,* 101, Wheaton: Harold Shaw Publishers.

30 Today's Gift daily emails, Hazelden Foundation, Scarf,

Maggie, *Secrets, Lies, Betrayals: The Body/Mind Connection,* Random House, 2004

31 Martin Luther Quotes: http://www.brainyquote.com/quotes/authors/m/martin_luther.html, accessed March 2005

32 *Mother Teresa Quotes:* http://www.brainyquote.com/quotes/authors/m/mother_teresa.html; accessed January 2005.

33 Jantz, Gregory L. *Hope, Help, and Healing for Eating Disorders,* 15, Wheaton: Harold Shaw Publishers, 1995.

34 Hooker, Sam and Adele, *Prayer and Other God Stuff,* 114, Portland: Ryan Gwinner Press, 1999

35 The Cybersalt Digest, *Today's Oneliner,* April 2006

36 The American Heritage Dictionary of the English Language, Fourth Edition Houghton Mifflin Company, 2003

37 Whitney, Dan and Wiseman, Neil, *Soulcare—New Every Morning,* June 8, 2006

38 Parham, A. Philip. 1993. Body, Mind and Soul, 1188, *Recovery Devotional Bible,* Grand Rapids: Zondervan.

39 Pope Gregory the Great, 6th-century a.d., first listed the seven deadly sins. The seven deadly sins, also known as the capital vices or cardinal sins, are a classification of vices used in early Christian teachings to educate and protect followers from basic human instincts; Accessed 05–20–2006, http://en.wikipedia.org/wiki/Seven_deadly_sins"

40 *Martin Luther Quotes,* http://www.brainyquote.com/quotes/authors/m/martin_luther.html, accessed March 2005

41 Stanley, Charles. 2005. *In Touch,* 7, January 2005, Atlanta: In Touch Ministries

42 Sheila Walsh, *The Heartache No One Sees,* 173,Nashville: Thomas Nelson, 2004

43 Gregory L. Jantz, *Hope, Help, and Healing for Eating Disorders,* 125, Wheaton: Harold Shaw Publishers 1995

44 Thomas, Gary L., *Authentic Faith,* 129, Grand Rapids: Zondervan, 2002

45 Used by Permission: *The Voice of the Martyrs,* htttp://www.persecution.com

46 Today's Gift daily emails, Hazelden Foundation

47 Oswald. 1963. What's the Good of Temptation? *My Utmost for His Highest,* September 17, Uhrichville: Barbour and Company.

48 Stanley, Charles. 2004. *In Touch,* 9, September 2004.

49 *Martin Luther Quotes,* http://www.brainyquote.com/quotes/authors/m/martin_luther.html, accessed March 2005

50 Partow Donna, *Becoming the Woman I Want to* Be, Minneapolis: Bethany House Publishers, 2004

51 Jantz, Gregory L. 1995. *Hope, Help, and Healing for Eating Disorders,* 141, Wheaton: Harold Shaw Publishers.

52 Jantz, Gregory L. 1995. *Hope, Help, and Healing for Eating Disorders,* 96, Wheaton: Harold Shaw Publishers.

53 Cited by Patrick Quillin. 1995. *Healing Secrets From the Bible,* 3, N. Canton: The Leader Company.

54 Patrick Quillin, PH.D, RD, CNS, *Healing Secrets From the Bible,* 5, The Leader Company, 1995

55 Dieting Quotes: http://en.thinkexist.com/quotations/dieting; accessed August 8, 2005

56 Jantz, Gregory L. 1998. *Spiritual Path to Weight Loss,* 11, Guideposts Books, Lincolnwood: Publications International.

57 Women's Body Image, National Women's Health Information Center, 1–800–994–9662, available from http://www.4woman.gov; accessed 6 November 2004.

58 Crabb, Larry, & Allender, Dan. 1996. *Hope When You're Hurting,* 194, 205, Grand Rapids: Zondervan Publishing House.

59 Mother Teresa Quotes: http://www.brainyquote.com/quotes/authors/m/mother_teresa.html

60 Chambers, Oswald. 1963. Missionary Predestinations, *My Utmost For His Highest,* September 21, Uhrichville: Barbour and Company.

61 *Serenity Prayer:* written by Reinhold Niebuhr, July 1, 1943 for the Union Church of Heath, Mass. It is used in Twelve-step programs today.

62 SoulCare New Every Morning, August 8, 2006

63 Marston, Ralph. The Daily Motivator, available at http://www.greatday.com; accessed 16 August 2004.

64. Beattie, Melody 1993. Live It Up!, 330, *Recovery Devotional Bible,* Grand Rapids: Zondervan.

65 Chambers, Oswald. 1963. Are You Fresh For Everything?, *My Utmost For His Highest,* January 20, Uhrichville: Barbour and Company.

66 The Quotation Page, http://www.quotationspage.com/quote/2755.html, accessed July 10, 2005

67 *St. Augustine Quotes:* http://www.brainyquote.com/quotes/authors/s/saint_augustine.html; accessed May, 2005

68 *The American Heritage Dictionary of the English Language, Fourth Edition, Houghton Mifflin Company, 2000*

69 *The Columbia Electronic Encyclopedia, Sixth Edition,* 2003, Columbia University Press. www.cc.columbia.edu/cu/cup, accessed July 20, 2006.

70 *The American Heritage Dictionary of the English Language, Fourth Edition*, Houghton Mifflin Company, 2004, www.answers.com/topic/thorn, accessed July 20, 2006.

71 Kendall, R. T. *A Thorn in the Flesh,* back cover, Lake Mary: Charisma House.

72 Lucado, Max. 2004. *In the Grip of Grace*, http://www.Christians-In-Recovery.com, December 14, 2004.

73 *Eating Disorders Review. PO Box 2238 Carlsbad, CA 92018, (800) 756–7533*

74 Gresham, Gayle L. *Today's Christian Woman* Magazine, Volume 27, Number 1, 2005, 39, Carol Stream: Illinois.

75 Focus on the Family. 1997. *The First Nine Months*, Colorado Springs, CO, 80995

76 Dr. Phil, ABC Television, www.drphil.com; accessed 3 November 2004.

77 Jones, Ann. *Next Time She'll Be Dead*, 87, Beacon Press, 1994.

78 Lifetime Television for Women, *Stop Violence Against Wom-*

en, http://www.lifetimetv.com/community/olc/violence/index. html; accessed 6 November 2004.

79 McCullough, Colleen. *The Thorn Birds*. 1980. Great Britain, accessed http://www.educa.rcanaria.es/usr/zonzamas/bird.htm, 16 January 2005.

All outside quotes that aren't referenced are from: daily sales quotes from justsell.com

TATE PUBLISHING & *Enterprises*

Tate Publishing is committed to excellence in the publishing industry. Our staff of highly trained professionals, including editors, graphic designers, and marketing personnel, work together to produce the very finest books available. The company reflects the philosophy established by the founders, based on Psalms 68:11,

"THE LORD GAVE THE WORD AND GREAT WAS THE COMPANY OF THOSE WHO PUBLISHED IT."

If you would like further information, please call
1.888.361.9473
or visit our website
www.tatepublishing.com

TATE PUBLISHING & *Enterprises*, LLC
127 E. Trade Center Terrace
Mustang, Oklahoma 73064 USA